BERLITZ PHRASE BOOKS

World's bestselling phrase books feature not only expressions and vocabulary you'll need, but also travel tips, useful facts and pronunciation throughout. The handiest and most readable conversation aid available.

Arabic	French	Polish
Chinese	German	Portuguese
Danish	Greek	Russian
Dutch	Hebrew	Serbo-Croatian
European	Hungarian	Spanish
(14 languages)	Italian	Lat.-Am. Spanish
European	Japanese	Swahili
Menu Reader	Korean	Swedish
Finnish	Norwegian	Turkish

BERLITZ CASSETTEPAKS

The above-mentioned titles are also available combined with a cassette to help you improve your accent. A helpful miniscript is included containing the complete text of the dual language hi-fi recording.

BERLITZ®

SWAHILI
FOR TRAVELLERS

By the staff of Berlitz Guides

Library of Congress Catalog Card Number: 73-20999

11th printing 1989

Printed in Switzerland

Berlitz Trademark Reg. U.S. Patent Office and other countries—Marca Registrada

Berlitz Guides
Avenue d'Ouchy 61
1000 Lausanne 6, Switzerland

Preface

You are about to visit East Africa. Our aim is to give you a new and more practical type of phrase book to help you on your trip.

Swahili for Travellers provides:

* all the phrases and supplementary vocabulary you will need on your trip

* a wide variety of tourist and travel facts, tips and useful information

* special sections showing the replies your listener might give to you. Just hand him the book and let him point to the appropriate phrase. This is especially practical in certain difficult situations (doctor, car mechanic, etc). It makes direct, quick and sure communication possible

* a logical system of presentation so that you can find the right phrase for the immediate situation

* quick reference through colour coding. The major features of the contents are on the back cover; a complete index is given inside.

These are just a few of the practical advantages. In addition, the book will prove a valuable introduction to life in East Africa.

There is a comprehensive section on Eating Out, giving translations and explanations for practically anything one would find on a menu in East Africa; there is a complete Shopping Guide that will enable you to obtain virtually anything you want. Trouble with the car? Turn to the mechanic's manual with its dual-language instructions. Feeling ill? Our medical section provides the most rapid communication possible between you and the doctor.

To make the most of *Swahili for Travellers,* we suggest that you start with the "Guide to Pronunciation". Then go on to "Some Basic Expressions". This not only gives you a minimum vocabulary; it helps you to pronounce the language.

There are differences in the usage of certain words between Uganda, Kenya and Tanzania, and sometimes even within the same country. Such differences may also occur depending upon how the noun is classified (see "Grammar"). We have tried to allow for that. Sometimes you will find alternatives for words given in brackets [] in the Swahili text. If your listener cannot understand your first expression, try the alternative in brackets.

We are particularly grateful to Mr. Nathanael Idarous, Mr. Frederick Kabuga, the Rev. Amon D. Mwakisunga, Mr. Edward J. Mwangosi and Mr. Migwe Thuo for their help in the preparation of this book, and also to Dr. T.J.A. Bennett for the "Guide to Pronunciation". We also wish to thank East African Airlines for its assistance.

We shall be very pleased to receive any comments, criticisms and suggestions that you think may help us in preparing future editions.

Thank you. Have a good trip.

Guide to pronunciation

Although a relatively easy language to pronounce, Swahili does require some effort on the part of the learner. But careful review of the indications given below will provide you with a solid basis for acquiring a good accent. Of course, the best guide is listening to native speakers in their day-to-day conversation. Pay particular attention to the sounds that are new to you, since these will be the most troublesome.

Originally, Swahili was written in Arabic characters. When British missionaries introduced our alphabet, they managed to adopt a transliteration as phonetic as possible. So you shouldn't find it too difficult to pronounce Swahili, especially if you carefully follow our explanations. As a minimum vocabulary for your trip, we have selected a number of basic words and phrases under the title "Some Basic Expressions" (pages 10–15).

Consonants

These are pronounced as in English, but the following points should be noted:

f	always as in few, never as in of	afya
g	always as in go, never as in gin	giza
m	this occurs frequently as a prefix for nouns, and in such cases it sounds as if it has a short oo sound in front of it, like the oo in look. *Note:* When m is followed by b or v, it is not preceded by the short oo sound and is not a separate syllable, except in words that contain only one vowel, e.g., mbu.	mpunga

PRONUNCIATION

n	as in English, but it can come before a consonant at the beginning of a word	**ndogo**
	Note: Before a vowel, **n** appears as **ny**, pronounced like **ni** in onion; e.g., **Nyasa** is pronounced **Nya-sa**, not **Ny-a-sa**.	
r	this letter is often confused in mainland speech with **l**	**rafiki**
s	always as in **so**, never as in vi**s**it	**hesabu**

Groups of consonants

th	always as in **th**in (in Arabic words only)	**thelathini**
dh	like **th** in **th**is	**dhuru**
gh	also comes from Arabic, but is only found in a few words. It is like the Scottish **ch** in lo**ch** but softer and voiced. It can also be pronounced as **g**. In most words, except for proper nouns, **kh** has been replaced by **h**.	**ghafula**
ng'	like **ng** in si**ng**er, NOT in fi**ng**er but it can come at the beginning of a word. You can produce the correct sound by dividing si**ng**er into si-**ng**er, and then practising the second syllable on its own.	**ng'a**
	Note: The **ng** sound in fi**ng**er is represented by **ng**, e.g., **nga**.	

Vowels

a	like **a** in **ah**	**paka**
e	like **ay** in m**ay**, but without the final **y** sound; it is a pure vowel, not a diphthong like English **ay**.	**enda**
i	like **ee** in m**ee**t	**fisi**

o	like **oa** in r**oa**st, but without a **w** sound at the end	**toka**
u	like **oo** in s**oo**t	**rudi**

N.B.

1) Unstressed vowels have the same quality as when they are stressed; therefore *paka* should not be pronounced like **parker**, rather the two *a*'s should have the same pronunciation.

2) When two vowels are next to each other, each retains its own pronunciation. Thus, *bei* is pronounced something like **bay**, *tai* like **tie,** *au* like the vowel in **cow.** In such cases the vowels are, in fact, separate syllables and the words could be divides *be-i, ta-i, a-u.*

3) When two similar vowels stand next to each other, they are pronounced as one long vowel, e.g., *kaa.*

4) Syllables in Swahili always end with a vowel, so a word like *pembeni* is divided *pe-mbe-ni.*

5) Stress is always on the next to the last syllable, except in one or two words borrowed from Arabic.

6) Intonation is more even than in English, and words are not emphasized in normal speech.

PRONUNCIATION

Some basic expressions

Yes.	**Ndiyo.**
No.	**Hapana[La].**
Please.*	**Tafadhali.**
Thank you.	**Asante.**
Thank you very much.	**Asante sana.**
That's all right.	**Vyema [Vema].**

Greetings

Jambo or *salamu* (hello) can be used at any time.

Good morning.	**Habari ya asubuhi.**
Good afternoon.	**Habari ya alasiri.**
Good evening.	**Habari za jioni.**
Good night.	**Lala salama.**
Good-bye.	**Kwa heri.**
See you later.	**Tutaonana baadaye.**
This is Mr. ...	**Huyu ni Bwana ...**
This is Mrs. ...	**Huyu ni Bibi ...**
This is Miss ...	**Huyu ni Bi. [Binti] ...**
I'm very pleased to meet you.	**Nimefurahi sana kukutana na wewe.**
How are you?	**U hali gani?**
Very well, thank you.	**Nzuri sana.**
And you?	**Na wewe, hujambo?**
Fine.	**Sijambo.**
Excuse me.	**Samahani.**

* Prefacing your request with *tafadhali* will add just the proper touch of politeness.

Questions

Where?	Wapi?
Where is ...?	Iko wapi...?
Where are ...?	Ziko wapi...?
When?	Lini?
What?	Nini?
How?	Vipi?
How much?	Bei gani?
How many?	Ngapi?
Who?	Nani?
Why?	Kwa nini?
Which?	Ipi?
What do you call this?	Hii inaitwa nini?
What do you call that?	Ile inaitwa nini?
What does this mean?	Maana ya hii ni nini?
What does that mean?	Maana ya ile ni nini?

Do you speak...?

Do you speak Arabic?	Unasema Kiarabu?
Do you speak English?	Unasema Kingereza?
Do you speak French?	Unasema Kifaransa?
Do you speak German?	Unasema Kijeremani?
Do you speak Swahili?	Unasema Kiswahili?
Could you speak more slowly, please?	Tafadhali, unaweza kusema taratibu zaidi?
Please point to the phrase in the book.	Tafadhali, onyesha hicho kifungu cha maneno kwenye kitabu.

Just a minute. I'll see if I can find it in this book.	**Subiri kidogo, niangalie kama nitakipata kwenye hiki kitabu.**
I understand.	**Naelewa.**
I don't understand.	**Sielewi.**

Can...?

Can I have ...?	**Naweza kupata ...?**
Can we have ...?	**Tunaweza kupata ...?**
Can you show me ...?	**Unaweza kunionyesha ...?**
Can you tell me ...?	**Unaweza kuniambia ...?**
Can you help me, please?	**Tafadhali, unaweza kunisaidia?**
Can you take me to ...?	**Unaweza kunipeleka ...?**

Wanting

I'd like ...	**Ningependa...**
We'd like ...	**Tungependa...**
Please give me ...	**Tafadhali nipe ...**
Give it to me, please.	**Nipatie hiyo, tafadhali.**
Please bring me ...	**Tafadhali niletee ...**
Bring it to me, please.	**Niletee hiyo, tafadhali.**
I'm hungry.	**Nina njaa.**
I'm thirsty.	**Nina kiu.**
I'm tired.	**Nimechoka.**
I'm lost.	**Nimepotea.**
It's important.	**Ni muhimu.**
It's urgent.	**Ni ya haraka.**
Hurry up!	**Harakisha!**

It is/There is...

There's no real Swahili translation of such expressions, which can only be used in full sentences:

It is ...	**Ni ...**
It's ...	**Ni ...**
Is it ...?	**Ndivyo...?**
It isn't ...?	**Sivyo**
There is ...	**Kuna ...**
There are ...	**Kuna [Pana] ...**
Is there ...?	**Kuna ...?**
Are there ...?	**Kuna ...?**
There isn't ...	**Hakuna ...**
There aren't...	**Hakuna ...**
There isn't any.	**Hakuna cho chote.**
There aren't any.	**Hakuna vyo vyote.**

A few common words

big	**kubwa**
small	**ndogo**
quick	**upesi**
slow	**pole pole**
early	**mapema**
late (to be late)	**·chelewa (kuchelewa)**
cheap	**rahisi**
expensive	**ghali**
near	**karibu**
far	**mbali**
hot	**moto**

cold	**baridi**
full	**-jaa**
empty	**tupu**
easy	**rahisi**
difficult	**-gumu**
heavy	**nzito**
light	**nyepesi**
open	**fungua**
shut	**funga**
right	**sawa**
wrong	**kosa**
old	**nzee**
new	**mpya**
old (of people)	**mzee**
young	**kijana**
beautiful	**-zuri**
ugly	**mbaya**
good	**bora**
bad	**mbaya [mbowu]**
better	**bora zaidi**
worse	**mbaya [mbovu] zaidi**

A few prepositions and some more useful words

at	**penye [kwenye]**
on	**juu ya**
in	**katika**
to	**kwa**
from	**kutoka**
inside	**ndani**

outside	**nje**
up	**juu**
down	**chini**
before	**kabla ya**
after	**baada ya**
with	**pamoja**
without	**bila [pasipo]**
through	**kupitia**
towards	**kuelekea**
until	**mpaka [hadi]**
during	**wakati wa**
and	**na**
or	**ama [au]**
not	**si [siyo]**
nothing	**si kitu**
none	**hamna**
very	**sana**
also	**pia**
soon	**punde**
perhaps	**labda [pengine]**
here	**hapa**
there	**kule, pale, huko**
now	**sasa**
then	**kisha**

A very basic grammar

Swahili is rapidly becoming the international language of Africa and thereby one of the important languages of the world. It's spoken primarily in Kenya, Tanzania and Uganda but it's also heard in parts of the neighbouring countries of Burundi, Malawi, Mozambique, Rwanda, Zaire and Zambia. That means that it's spoken by roughly 35–40 million people.

Actually, the name "swahili" isn't African at all but Arabic and means "coasts" for originally Swahili was the language of the East African coast. There are several dialects of Swahili and differences in usage depending upon the region but the leading version is that of Zanzibar which is the basis of standard Swahili.

Swahili belongs to the Bantu family of languages and is part of the group of languages spoken in central, eastern and southern Africa. But throughout history, traders and settlers—mainly Arab and European—coming to the East African coasts have greatly influenced the language spoken there. Moreover, it was originally only a spoken language and was subsequently put into a written form by foreigners who thus influenced the tongue. Mainly the Arabs and the English have left their imprint on present-day Swahili.

Learning Swahili isn't at all like learning French, German or Spanish. When we try to learn another European language, the first thing we're concerned with is the vocabulary and then the grammatical forms. After learning vocabulary, we must next become familiar with conjugations, declensions and, to a lesser extent, word order. With Swahili the problem of vocabulary remains, but the grammar itself is much easier.

The structure is quite simple: verbs, nouns, adjectives and adverbs often all come from the same basic root. The same thing frequently occurs in English. Take the word "child": from it we can compose other words (nouns, adjectives, adverbs) like children, childhood, childlike, childishly. The basic root for all these words is "child", and different words can be made by adding suffixes which indicate the precise meanings of the new words. Swahili has basically the same structure, but in order to form a word we don't add a suffix but a *prefix*. The prefix is the most important characteristic of Swahili grammar. Prefixes are used not only to indicate the singular and plural of nouns and the tenses of the verbs, and to form adjectives, adverbs, and pronoun objects, but many other things as well.

Nouns

Nouns in Swahili aren't preceded by definite or indefinite articles (a, an, the). The meaning is understood from the context.

Nouns in Swahili don't have a gender but they belong to *classes;* each class consists of nouns of a certain type (e.g., abstract concepts, living things, human beings). There are eight such classes. In each of them the nouns take a different sort of prefix. For example, the word **kitu** (thing) belongs to the **ki**-class, but the word **mtu** (man) belongs to the **m**-class. If you really want to learn Swahili well, it's always best to learn the word and the class it belongs to together as you'd learn in French whether a word is masculine or feminine.

Here's a basic list showing the eight classes of nouns. Note that the prefixes shown are subject to numerous exceptions especially when they precede words starting with a vowel.

Class of nouns	Sing. prefix	Plural prefix	Examples	
1. Human beings	**m-** or **mw-**	**wa-** or **w-**	**mtoto** **watoto**	child children
2. a) Inanimate objects; b) plants	**m-** or **mw-** or **mu-**	**mi-**	**mti** **miti**	tree trees
3. Miscellaneous	**n-** (often dropped)	**n-** (often dropped)	**nyumba**	house/ houses
4. Inanimate objects	**ki-** or **ch-**	**vi-** or **vy-**	**kiko** **viko**	pipe pipes
5. Miscellaneous	–	**ma-**	**ua** **maua**	flower flowers
6. Words without a plural: abstract concepts, names of countries, etc.	**u-**	–	**(-refu** **urefu**	long) length
7. One word only: **mahali**	in agreements: **pa-**	in agreements: **pa-**	**mahali** **pazuri**	a nice place
8. Verbs used as nouns	**ku-**	–	**kuandika**	to write, writing

Adjectives

The basic rule is that the class prefix of the noun is also added to the adjective that modifies it.

The adjective always follows the noun it modifies. It agrees in class and number with the noun except in the case of adjectives derived from Arabic which are all invariable.

Example:

kitu	thing
-dogo	small
kitu kidogo	a small thing

Even if the prefix of the noun has been dropped (as is the case in the **n**-class), the adjective will still take the prefix. However, here again, the prefix rule is quite complicated and there are many exceptions.

Numerals are considered as adjectives so they also take the class prefix except for numbers six, seven, nine and decimal numbers.

Example:		
	kitabu	the book
	vitabu	the books
	-tano	five
	vitabu vitano	five books

Adverbs

Most adverbs have one single form which doesn't change and doesn't take a prefix. Some examples:

nyuma	behind
ndani	inside
nje	outside
karibu	nearby
sasa	now

But adverbs can also be formed from adjectives and nouns:

-zuri	nice
vizuri	nicely
askari	soldier
kiaskari	like a soldier

Verbs

The verb has to agree with the subject noun by taking the same prefix. When the subject of a verb isn't a noun, but what we call a personal pronoun, Swahili verbs again take a prefix. Here they are:

Singular		Plural	
I	**ni-**	we	**tu-**
you	**u-**	you	**m-**
he, she	**a-**	they	**wa-**

The tenses are *also* indicated by prefixes. They're inserted between the subject prefix and the root of the verb. These prefixes denoting the tenses are: **-na-** for the present tense, **-li-** for the past tense, and **-ta-** for future tense.

Examples:

ni/na/soma	I'm reading
ni/ta/soma	I shall read
a/li/soma	he read
wa/na/soma	they're reading
wa/ta/soma	they'll read
tu/li/soma	we read

Kisu kimoja kitatosha.   One knife will do.

The **-na-** tense is basically a continuous present. There's another present tense which takes the prefix **-a-** and has no particular sense of time attached to it.

Prefixes are also used to indicate the direct object of the verb. They're the same as the subject prefixes and are often used even if the object noun itself is also expressed in the sentence. For example: **nilikisoma** (I read it). When referring to persons, the object prefixes are:

Singular		Plural	
me	-ni-	us	-tu-
you	-ku-	you	-wa-
him, her	-m-	them	-wa-

In order to ask a question in Swahili, the word order of the sentence doesn't change. Questions are understood from the intonation.

In the present tense the verb to be is dropped, and only the personal prefix is used. Examples:

U imara.   You're strong.
Yu tayari.   He's ready.

The verb to have is expressed in the present tense by the pronoun followed by **-na.**

Examples:

nina	I've	**tuna**	we've
una	you've	**mna**	you've
ana	he/she has	**wana**	they've

The negative form in this tense again uses the suffix **-na** with a negative pronoun:

Examples:

sina	I haven't	**hatuna**	we haven't
huna	you haven't	**hamnayo**	you haven't
hana	he/she hasn't	**hawana**	they haven't

Demonstratives

Demonstratives, whether they're used as adjectives (this/that house) or as pronouns (this/that is good), are rendered by means of **hi-/ha-/hu-,** etc. (this, these), or **-le** (that, those). The form varies according to class.

Here's the table of demonstratives:

Class:	1	2	3	4	5	6	7	8
this these	**huyu** **hawa**	**huu** **hii**	**hii** **hizi**	**hiki** **hivi**	**hili** **haya**	**huu** **hizi**	**hapa** –	**huku** –
that those	**yule** **wale**	**ule** **ile**	**ile** **zile**	**kile** **vile**	**lile** **yale**	**ule** **zile**	**pale** –	**kule** –

For example:

mtu huyu	this man
watu hawa	these men
kitu kile	that thing
vitu vile	those things

Arrival

Passport control

There's certain to be somebody around who speaks English. That's why we're making this a brief section.

Here's my passport.	**Hii hapa pasi yangu.**
I'll be staying …	**Nitakaa …**
a few days	**siku chache**
a week	**wiki moja**
two weeks	**wiki mbili**
a month	**mwezi mmoja**
I don't know yet.	**Sijui bado.**
I'm here on holiday.	**Nipo hapa kwa likizo.**
I'm here on business.	**Nipo hapa kwa shughuli.**
I'm just passing through.	**Napita njia tu.**

If things become difficult:

I'm sorry, I don't understand.	**Samahani, sielewi.**
Is there anyone here who speaks English?	**Yupo mtu yeyote hapa anayesema Kiingereza?**

Note: You should check with your travel agent and the embassies or consulates of the countries you wish to visit about visa and vaccination requirements. Medical progress has put a halt to grave diseases and illnesses which once plagued the region. Yellow fever and cholera inoculations are advisable, but obligatory only if you enter from an infected area.

FOR CAR/BORDER FORMALITIES, see page 146

Customs

It is illegal to import local currencies. Foreign exchange earning is the basis for the promotion of tourism in the different countries you are likely to visit and you may have to pay for certain goods and services in US$, £Stg., DM or SFr. All foreign currency must be declared on arrival. You'll be able to take out up to the amounts declared.

The chart below shows what you can bring in duty-free to East African countries.*

	cigarettes		cigars		tobacco	liquor
Kenya Tanzania Uganda	200	or	50	or	½ lb.	1 bottle 1 bottle ¼ gal.

I've nothing to declare.	**Sina cho chote cha kulipia ushuru.**
I've ...	**Ninayo ...**
a carton of cigarettes	**kasha la sigara**
a bottle of whisky	**chupa ya wiski**
Must I pay on this?	**Itanibidi kuilipia hii?**
How much?	**Kiasi gani?**
It's for my personal use.	**Ni ya matumizi yangu pekee.**
It's not new.	**Si mpya.**

ARRIVAL

* All allowances subject to change without notice.

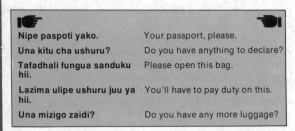

Nipe paspoti yako.	Your passport, please.
Una kitu cha ushuru?	Do you have anything to declare?
Tafadhali fungua sanduku hii.	Please open this bag.
Lazima ulipe ushuru juu ya hii.	You'll have to pay duty on this.
Una mizigo zaidi?	Do you have any more luggage?

Baggage—Porters

The porter may take your luggage through customs for you. He'll then wait till it's been cleared. Note the number on his badge.

Porter!	**Mchukuzi!**
Please take these bags.	**Chukua masanduku haya.**
That's mine.	**Hilo ni langu.**
That's my ...	**Hilo ni ... langu**
bag/luggage/suitcase	**shanta/mzigo/sanduku**
That ... one.	**Lile ...**
big/small	**kubwa/dogo**
blue/brown/black	**buluu/kunde/jeusi**
There's one piece missing.	**Kitu kimoja kimepotea.**
Take this bag to the ...	**Chukua begi hili kwa ...**
bus/taxi	**basi/teksi**
I'm looking for porter 7.	**Namtafuta hamali nambari 7.**
How much is that?	**Ni kiasi gani?**

Note: A fair tip in East Africa is 5 to 10 shillings. Some ports and airports have fixed charges for porters. Have some small change ready.

ARRIVAL

Changing money

You'll find a banking service or a currency exchange office at most airports. If it's closed, don't worry. You'll be able to change money at your hotel.

Full details about money and currency exchange are given on page 134.

Where's the nearest currency-exchange office?	Ni wapi karibu pa kubadilishia fedha?
Can you change these traveller's cheques (checks)?	Unaweza kubadilisha hizi cheki za safari?
I want to change some ...	Nataka kubadilisha ...
dollars	dola za Kimarekani
pounds	pauni za Kiingereza
Can you change this into East African shillings?	Je unaweza kuzibadilisha hizi katika shilingi za Afrika mashariki?
What's the exchange rate for a pound/for a dollar?	Ni kiasi gani cha kubadilishia pauni moja/dola moja?

Directions

How do I get to ...?	(Vipi nitafika ...?) Nitafikaje ...?
Where's the bus into town?	Basi linalokwenda mjini liko wapi?
Where can I get a taxi?	Nitapatia wapi teksi?
Where can I rent a car?	Nitakodisha gari wapi?

Hotel reservations

Many terminals have a hotel reservation service or tourist information office. You're sure to find someone there who speaks English. There may be a small charge for reservations.

Car hire (rental)

Again it's best to make arrangements in advance whenever possible. There are car hire (rental) firms at most airports and terminals. When asking for a car, specify that you want to drive it yourself. It's likely that someone there will speak English. But if nobody does, try one of the following:

I'd like a ...	**Ningependa ...**
car	**gari**
small car	**gari ndogo**
large car	**gari kubwa**
sports car	**gari ya spoti**
I'd like it for ...	**Naitaka kwa ...**
a day/four days	**siku moja/siku nne**
a week/two weeks	**wiki moja/wiki mbili**
What's the charge per ...	**Ni kiasi gani kwa ...**
day/week	**siku moja/wiki**
Does that include mileage?	**Hiyo ni pamoja na malipo kwa kilometa?**
What's the charge per kilometre?	**Ni kiasi gani kwa kila kilometa?**
Is petrol (gasoline) included?	**Hiyo ni pamoja na petroli?**
I want a full insurance.	**Nataka bima kamili.**
What's the deposit?	**Amana ni kiasi gani?**
I've a credit card.	**Nina kadi ya benki.**
Here's my driving licence.	**Hiki cheti changu cha kuendeshea gari.**

Note: To drive in East Africa, you'll need an international driving licence. In all East African countries you drive on the left-hand side of the road.

FOR SIGHTSEEING, see page 75

ARRIVAL

Taxi

Practically all taxis have meters. It's usually best to ask the approximate fare beforehand. For some trips (e.g., airport to town) there may be a fixed rate. This will be posted at the airport.

Although the tip is included in the fare, it's common practice to round off upwards to the nearest shilling.

Where can I get a taxi?	**Wapi nitapata teksi?**
Please get me a taxi.	**Tafadhali niletee teksi.**
What's the fare to ...?	**Nauli ni kiasi gani kwenda ...?**
How far is it to ...?	**Umbali gani kwenda ...?**
Take me to ...	**Nipeleke kwa ...**
this address	**anuani hii**
the town centre	**mjini**
the ... Hotel	**... Hotel**
Turn ... at the next corner.	**Pinda ... kwenye kona ijayo.**
left/right	**kushoto/kulia**
Go straight ahead.	**Nenda moja kwa moja.**
Please stop here.	**Simama hapa.**
I'm in a hurry.	**Mimi nina haraka.**
There's no hurry.	**Hapana haraka.**
Could you drive more slowly?	**Unaweza kuendesha pole pole?**
Could you help me to carry my bags?	**Unaweza kunisaidia kuchukua mizigo yangu?**

Hotel—Other accommodation

Early reservation—and confimation—is recommended in major tourist centres during the high season. Most towns have a tourist information office—and that's the place to go if you're stuck without a room.

There's no standard accommodation classification for all of East Africa. In tourist resorts there are only luxury and first-class hotels. But, as a general rule, the following categories of accommodation are to be found in the major cities:

Luxury	As the name implies.
1st class	All facilities; all with private bath and toilet; telephone, radio and television.
2nd class	Comfortable, good service; most rooms with showers.
3rd class	Services limited.
Motels	While there are very few, they do offer the motorist good accommodation, good food, and many other services in a pleasant atmosphere.
Nyumba ya wageni	Guest or boarding houses: normally for a stay of several weeks or even months; offering board according to requirements.
Kijumba chenye vyombo vyote	Furnished bungalows: they're usually located near a beach. Ask about them at the tourist office. They sometimes also adjoin large hotels.
Kitanda na chakula cha asubuhi	Bed and breakfast: watch for signs placed at the roadside by families who offer such accommodation. The proprietor often places more importance on having your friendship than on the sum of money you'll pay him.

HOTEL

In this section, we're mainly concerned with the smaller and medium-priced hotels and boarding houses. You'll have no language difficulties in the luxury and first-class hotels where most of the staff speak English.

In the next few pages we consider your requirements —step by step—from arrival to departure. You needn't read through the whole lot; just turn to the situation that applies.

Checking in—Reception

My name is ...	Jina langu ni ...
I've a reservation.	Nimethabitisha agizo.
We've reserved two rooms, a single and a double.	Tumeagiza vyumba viwili, cha mtu pekee na cha watu wawili.
I wrote to you last month.	Nilikuandikia mwezi uliopita.
Here's the confirmation.	Hii hapa thibitisho.
I'd like ...	Ningependa ...
a single room	chumba cha mtu pekee
a double room	chumba cha watu wawili
two single rooms	vyumba viwili vya mtu pekee
a room with twin beds	chumba chenye vitanda viwili
a room with a bath	chumba chenye bafu
a room with a shower	chumba chenya bomba la maji ya rasharasha
a room with a balcony	chumba chenye roshani
a room with a view	chumba chenye mandhari
a suite	chumba kamili ya nyumba
We'd like a room ...	Tungependa chumba kiliopo ...
in the front	mbele
at the back	nyuma
facing the sea	kukabili bahari
facing the courtyard	kukabili uwanja
It must be quiet.	Lazima kiwe kimya.

HOTEL

Is there ...?	Kuna ...? [Ipo ...?]
air conditioning	air condition
heating	mtambo wa joto
a radio	radio
a television	televisheni
laundry service	utumishi wa dobi
room service	utumishi wa chumbani
hot water	maji ya moto
running water	maji ya bomba
a private toilet	choo cha binafsi

How much?

What's the price ...?	Ni kiasi gani?
per week	kwa wiki moja
per night	kwa usiku mmoja
for bed and breakfast	kwa kulala na chakula cha asubuhi
excluding meals	bila ya vyakula
for full board	kulala na vyakula vyote
for half board	kwa kulala na baadhi ya vyakula
Does that include...?	Hesabu hiyo pamoja na...?
breakfast	chakula cha asubuhi
meals	vyakula
service	utumishi
tax	kodi
Is there any reduction for children?	Pana upungufu wa malipo kwa watoto?
Do you charge for the baby?	Unamlipisha mtoto mchanga pia?
That's too expensive.	Hiyo ni ghali sana.
Haven't you anything cheaper?	Huna kitu chochote rahisi?

HOTEL

FOR NUMBERS, see page 175

How long?

We'll be staying...	**Tutakaa...**
overnight only	**usiku mmoja tu**
a few days	**siku chache**
(at least) a week	**(kama) wiki moja**
I don't know yet.	**Sijui bado.**

Decision

May I see the room?	**Naweza kukiona chumba?**
No, I don't like it.	**Hapana, sikipendi.**
It's too...	**Kina ... sana.**
cold/hot	**baridi/joto**
dark/small	**giza/udogo**
noisy	**kelele**
I asked for a room with a bath.	**Nilitaka chumba chenye bafu.**
Do you have anything ...?	**Una kitu chochote...?**
better/bigger	**bora/kikubwa**
cheaper/quieter	**rahisi/kimya zaidi**
higher up/lower down	**juu zaidi/chini kabisa**
Do you have a room with a better view?	**Unacho chumba chenye mandhari bora?**
That's fine. I'll take it.	**Hicho kitafaa. Nitakichukua.**

HOTEL

Bills

These are usually paid weekly or upon departure if you stay less than a week. Most hotels offer a reduction of 50% for children under 12.

FOR DAYS OF THE WEEK, see page 180

Tipping

If you appreciate a service, tip at your discretion, but keep it moderate. Most good hotels and restaurants include a ten-percent service charge in the bill.

Is service included? **Eti pamoja na utumishi?**

Registration

Upon arrival at a hotel or boarding house you'll be asked to fill in a registration form *(maandikisho)*. It asks for your name, home address, passport number and further destination. It's certain to carry an English translation.

What does this mean? **Nini maana ya hii?**

The desk-clerk will probably ask you for your passport. He may want to keep it for a while, even overnight. Don't worry. You'll get it back. He may want to ask you the following questions:

Naweza kuona pasi yako?	May I see your passport?
Utajali kujaza orodha hii ya kawaida?	Would you mind filling in this registration form?
Tafadhali, weka sahihi yako hapa.	Please sign here.
Je, utakaa kwa muda gani?	How long will you be staying?

What's my room number? **Chumba changu nambari ngapi?**

Will you have our bags sent up? **Unaweza kutuletea mizigo yetu juu?**

Service, please

Now that you're safely installed, meet some more of the hotel staff:

bellboy	mtumishi mlangoni
maid	msaidizi wa kike
manager	meneja [msimamizi]
room service	utumishi chumbani
switchboard operator	mtumishi wa simu
waiter	mwandishi [mtumishi]
waitress	mwandishi wa kike

Call the members of the staff *bibi* (miss), *mama* (madam) or *bwana* (sir) when calling for service.

General requirements

Please ask the maid to come up.	Tafadhali mwite msaidizi wa kike aje hapa.
Who is it?	Nani?
Just a minute.	Ngoja kidogo.
Come in!	Ingia!
The door's open.	Mlango u wazi.
Is there a bath on this floor?	Lipo bafu katika ghorofa hii?
How does this shower work?	Vipi unaendeshwa mfereji huu wa kuogea?
Where's the plug for the shaver?	Ipo wapi plagi ya mashini ya kunyolea?
What's the voltage here?	Nguvu ya umeme ni ngapi hapa?
Can we have breakfast in our room?	Tunaweza kupata chakula cha asubuhi chumbani?
I'd like to leave these in your safe.	Napenda kuweka hivi katika dhamana yako.
Can you find me a baby-sitter?	Unaweza kunipatia msaidizi wa kutazama mtoto?

May I have a/an/some...?	Naweza kupata ...?
ashtray	bakuli la majivu
bath towel	tauli ya kuogea
extra blanket	blanketi zaidi
envelopes	bahasha za barua
(more) hangers	vitundikia nguo (zaidi)
ice cubes	vipande vya barafu
extra pillow	mto wa kulalia zaidi
reading-lamp	taa ya kusomea
soap	sabuni
writing paper	karatasi ya kuandikia

Where's the ...?	Wapi ...?
barber's	kwa kinyozi
bathroom	chumba cha kuogea
beauty parlour	duka la mapambo
cocktail lounge	ukumbi wa vinywaji
dining-room	chumba cha kulia
hairdresser's	kwa kinyozi wa kike
restaurant	mkahawa
television room	chumba cha televisheni
toilet	choo

Breakfast

An East African breakfast consists of bread and butter, sometimes beans and tea. Some restaurants serve omelets for breakfast. However, most hotels can also provide an English or American breakfast.

I'll have a/an/some ...	Nataka ...
bacon and eggs	nyama ya bacon na mayai
beans	maharagwe
cereals	nafaka
hot/cold	moto/baridi
eggs	mayai
boiled egg	yai lililochemshwa
soft/medium/hard	laini/wastani/gumu
fried eggs	kimanda
scrambled eggs	mayai yaliyovurugwa

HOTEL SERVICE

fruit juice	maji ya matunda
grapefruit/orange	mabalungi/machungwa
pineapple/tomato	nanasi/nyanya
ham and eggs	nyama ya ham na mayai
jam	mraba
marmalade	mraba ya machungwa
omelet	kimanda
pancakes	mkate wa upawa
toast	tosti, mkate uliokaushwa
yoghurt	mtindi wa maziwa

May I have some …?	Nataka …
hot/cold milk	maziwa ya moto/baridi
cream/sugar	mafuta ya maziwa/sukari
bread/rolls	mkate/mkate wa kusukuma
butter	siagi
salt/pepper	chumvi/pilipili manga
coffee/tea	kahawa/chai
chocolate	chakleti ya kunywa
lemon/honey	ndimu/asali
hot water	maji ya moto

Could you bring me a …?	Unaweza kuniletea …?
plate	sahani
glass/cup	bilauri/kikombe
knife/fork	kisu/uma
spoon	kijiko

HOTEL SERVICE

Difficulties

The … doesn't work.	… haifanyi kazi.
air-conditioner	air condition
fan	kipepeo
heating	mtambo wa joto
light	taa
radio	radio
tap	bomba
toilet	choo
ventilator	kipepeo cha hewa safi

FOR EATING OUT, see pages 38–64

The wash-basin is clogged.	**Bafu limeziba.**
The window is jammed.	**Dirisha limeganda.**
The blind is stuck.	**Kipaa cha jua kimesita.**
These aren't my shoes.	**Hivi si viatu vyangu.**
This isn't my laundry.	**Hizi si nguo zangu.**
There's no hot water.	**Hapana maji ya moto.**
I've lost my watch.	**Nimepoteza saa yangu.**
I've left my key in my room.	**Nimesahau ufunguo wangu ndani ya chumba.**
The ... is broken/ burnt out.	**... imevunjika.**
bulb	**globu ya taa**
lamp	**taa**
plug	**plagi**
shutter	**pazia**
switch	**swichi ya taa**
venetian blind	**kipaa cha jua**
window shade	**pazia la dirisha**
The mosquito net is torn.	**Chandalua kimetatuka.**
Can you get it repaired?	**Unaweza kukitengeneza?**

Telephone—Mail—Callers

Can you get me Kampala 12345?	**Unaweza kunipatia simu Kampala 12345?**
Did anyone telephone me?	**Kuna mtu yeyote aliyenipigia simu?**
Do you have any stamps?	**Unauza stempu?**
Would you please mail this for me?	**Kwa hisani yako nitilie hii posta.**
Are there any messages for me?	**Kuna maagizo yeyote kwangu?**

FOR POST OFFICE and TELEPHONE, see pages 137–141

Checking out

May I please have my bill?	**Tafadhali nipe hesabu yangu.**
I'm leaving early tomorrow. Please have my bill ready.	**Nitaondoka kesho mapema. Tafadhali weka hesabu yangu tayari.**
We'll be checking out around noon/soon.	**Tutafutisha wakati wa mchana/baadaye kidogo.**
I must leave at once.	**Lazima niondoke hivi sasa.**
Is everything included?	**Hii ni hesabu ya kila kitu?**
You've made a mistake in this bill, I think.	**Umefanya makosa katika hesabu hii, nafikiri.**
Can you get us a taxi?	**Unaweza kutupatia teksi?**
When's the next ... to Dar es Salaam?	**Wakati gani ... ijayo itakwenda Dar es-Salaam?**
bus/train/plane	**basi/gari la moshi/ndege**
Would you send someone to bring down our baggage?	**Unaweza kumtuma mtu atuletee mizigo yetu hapa chini?**
We're in a great hurry.	**Sisi tuna haraka sana.**
Here's the forwarding address.	**Hii ni anuani yangu ya mahali niendapo.**
You have my home address.	**Unayo anuani yangu ya nyumbani.**
It's been a very enjoyable stay.	**Tumefurahishwa sana na makaazi yetu.**
I hope we'll come again sometime.	**Nataraji tutakuja mara nyingine baadaye.**

HOTEL SERVICE

FOR TAXI, see page 27

Eating out

You'll find that in East African cities the food is influenced by Arab and Indian cooking. In the coastal regions you'll enjoy dishes prepared with coconut milk instead of plain water and spiced with cloves and red pepper. Inland, the food is noted for being simple but tasty.

Only a few restaurants serve alcoholic beverages but beer can be found everywhere.

Baa	Bar: serves drinks and appetizers.
Baraza	Local café: usually open-air or at the balcony of a restaurant where people pass their time playing games or chatting while sipping their tea or coffee. Don't hesitate to join them.
Mkahawa	Small café, serving mainly non-alcoholic drinks; varied menus. Sit at the counter or choose a table for the same price. The *sahani ya leo* (set menu) is often surprisingly good. In local *mikahawa*, you only find local specialities.
Baa ya dansi	Dance bar: serves alcoholic and non-alcoholic drinks. Just choose your music from a juke-box. These dance bars—found only in the cities—are usually reasonably priced. Some may charge an entrance fee.
Mahali pa mshikaki	An open-air stand selling *mshikaki* (pieces of beef roasted on a skewer and served with salad). Some also serve *mtabakiya* (double pancakes stuffed with a spiced omelet).
Chumba cha chai	Tearoom or snack-bar: serves hot and cold non-alcoholic drinks, Indian *badjias* (small cereal rolls) with pickled chutney.

Mkahawa wa baniani	Vegetarian restaurant: serves Indian *puri* (light rolls), rice and vegetable curry, several kinds of beans, plenty of yoghurt and fresh fruit.

Mealtimes

Breakfast *(chakula cha asubuhi)* is served from 7 until 9.30 a.m.

Lunch *(chakula cha mchana)* is the main meal in East Africa; it's served from about noon until 2.30 p.m.

Dinner *(chakula cha jioni)* is served from 7 to 9.30 p.m.

However, these mealtimes go for hotel restaurants only. Food stands and similar places serve meals virtually all day long until midnight and even later. Some restaurants close one day per week.

In this section, we're primarily concerned with lunch and dinner. We assume that you had breakfast at your hotel. (For a breakfast menu, see page 34.)

Eating habits

East African eating habits are simple and to the point. Most local people use their fingers for eating; they believe that using any instrument other than your own fingers for eating spoils the taste of the food.

However, in hotel restaurants you can expect a European style of dining, which will present no problems. At local restaurants you may have to ask for some cutlery, though a spoon will be provided in any case. Don't be put off if you're not provided with a serviette (napkin); local custom prefers the use of the washbasin and towel which every restaurant has.

EATING OUT

During the hot season you're likely to need more drinking water than you normally do. The waiter is very well aware of this and will refill your glass the moment it's empty. Otherwise, ask him to bring you *maji baridi* (iced water). In remote areas you'd be advised to have your water boiled or put special tablets into it.

In a country where fresh fruit is plentiful you'd probably prefer to eat fruit after your meal rather than a sweet dessert. Fruit is either placed on the table, or you name it and they'll get it for you. If it isn't sweet enough ask for *sukari* (sugar).

You might be treated to a meal sometime. When you've finished the main course, your host may insist on offering you more. If you're absolutely sure you've reached your limit, say *asante, lakini siwezi kula zaidi* (thank you, but I can't eat any more).

Hungry?

I'm hungry/I'm thirsty.	**Nina njaa/Nina kiu.**
Can you recommend a good restaurant?	**Unaweza kunisifia mkahawa mzuri?**
Are there any inexpensive restaurants around here?	**Ipo mikahawa ya rahisi hapa karibu?**

If you want to be sure of getting a table in one of the better-known restaurants, it may be advisable to telephone in advance.

I'd like to reserve a table for four.	**Napenda kuagiza meza kwa watu wanne.**
We'll come at 8.	**Tutakuja saa 8.**

Asking and ordering

Good evening. I'd like a table for three.	**Habari za jioni. Napenda kupata meza ya watu watatu.**
Could we have a ...?	**Tunaweza kupata ...?**
table in the corner	**meza iliopo pembeni**
table by the window	**meza karibu na dirisha**
table outside	**meza iliopo nje**
Where are the toilets?	**Vipo wapi vyoo?**
May I please have the menu?	**Nipe orodha ya vyakula.**
What's this?	**Nini hii?**
Do you have ....?	**Unayo ...?**
a set menu	**orodha maalum ya vyakula**
local dishes	**vyakula vya nchini**
I'd like ...	**Nitapenda ...**
Is service included?	**Pamoja na ijara ya utumishi?**
Could we have (a/an) ..., please?	**Unaweza kutuletea ...?**
ashtray	**bakuli la majivu**
another chair	**kiti kingine**
fork	**uma**
glass	**bilauri**
knife	**kisu**
napkin	**kitambaa cha kulia**
plate	**sahani**
serviette	**kitambaa cha kulia**
spoon	**kijiko**
toothpick	**kijiti cha meno**

EATING OUT

Utapenda nini?	What would you like?
Hii ni bora.	I recommend this.
Utapenda kunywa nini?	What would you like to drink?
Unataka ...?	Do you want ...?

FOR COMPLAINTS, see page 59

I'd like a/an/some ...	Nitapenda ...
aperitif	kinywaji kabla ya chakula
appetizer	kitamshaji [vitamshaji]
beer	bia [pombe]
bread	mkate
butter	siagi
cabbage	mboga ya kebeji
chips	viazi vya kukaangwa
cheese	jibini
coffee	kahawa
dessert	chakula mwisho
fish	samaki
french fries	viazi vya kukaangwa
fruit	matunda
game	nyama ya mnyama wa porini
ice-cream	barafu ya kirimu
ketchup	achali ya nyanya
lemon	ndimu
lettuce	figili
meat	nyama
milk	maziwa
mustard	haradali
oil	mafuta
olive oil	mafuta ya zeituni
pepper	pilipili manga
potatoes	viazi ulaya
poultry	kuku
rice	wali
rolls	mkate wa kusukuma
salad	saladi
salt	chumvi
sandwich	mkate uliojazwa nyama
seafood	aina za samaki wa baharini
seasoning	kiungo cha mchuzi
soup	supu
spaghetti	spageti
starter	chakula cha mwanzo
sugar	sukari
tea	chai
vegetables	mboga
vinegar	siki
(iced) water	maji (ya barafu)
wine	mvinyo

What's on the menu?

Our menu is presented according to courses. Under the headings below you'll find alphabetical lists of dishes that might be offered on an East African menu with their English equivalent. You can also show the book to the waiter. If you want some fruit, for instance, show him the appropriate list and let him point to what's available. Use pages 41 and 42 for ordering in general.

Here then is our guide to good eating and drinking. Turn to the section you want.

EATING OUT

Obviously, you're not going to go through every course.

Nothing more, thanks.   **Nimeshiba, asante.**

East African food is very tasty and offers a wide range of specialities, which vary from country to country, often from place to place.

Appetizers

Appetizers play an important part in East African cooking. They range from simple dishes of olives, freshly-roasted cashews and roasted cassava roots to creations that are a meal in themselves.

I'd like an appetizer. What do you recommend?	**Nataka vichangamshaji. Nini utanisifia?**
biringani	aubergine (eggplant)
chaza	mussels
embe (mbichi)	(raw) mango
kamba	lobster
kamba wa mtoni	crayfish
kanju	cashew fruit
korosho	cashew nuts
maini ya kuku	chicken livers
maji ya matunda	fruit juice
mabalungi/machungwa	grapefruit/orange
nanasi/nyanya	pineapple/tomato
matango	cucumber
mayai yaliotokoswa sana	hard-boiled eggs
mayai ya samaki	caviar
mboga ya kitete	asparagus
mhogo	cassava
mkunga	eel
mkunga iliokaushwa	smoked eel
nyama baridi	cold meat
nyama ya kaa	crab meat
paja la nguruwe	ham
paja la nguruwe iliotokoswa	boiled ham
paja la nguruwe liliokaushwa	smoked ham
samaki tamvu	herring
samaki tamvu waliokaushwa	smoked herring
samaki tamvu na ukwaju	herring marinated in citrus juice
tikiti maji	melon
tini (kavu)	(dry) figs
uyoga	mushrooms
zeituni	olives
zeituni zenye pilipili	stuffed olives

Salads

What salads do you have?	**Una saladi aina gani?**
Can you recommend a local speciality?	**Unaweza kunisifia saladi ya mahali?**

biringani iliyokaushwa	smoked bringal (eggplant)
nyanya zilizokaushwa na nanaa	smoked tomato and mint
saladi ya figili	lettuce salad
saladi ya majani	green salad
saladi ya mbatata	potato salad
saladi ya mzizi wa figili	radish salad
saladi ya tango	cucumber salad

Egg dishes and omelets

I'd like an omelet.	**Nataka kimand.**

kimanda cha kamba kamba	shrimp omelet
kimanda chenye viungo	spiced omelet
kimanda na nyanya	tomato omelet
mayai ya kutokoswa	boiled eggs
mayai ya kukaangwa	fried eggs
mayai ya kuchemshwa	poached eggs
mayai ya kuvurugwa	scrambled eggs
mayai yaliyotokoswa laini	soft-boiled eggs

Some coastal restaurants serve an omelet on a bed of rice *(andazi la mayai juu ya wali)*. An omelet is normal breakfast fare in East Africa.

Other egg dishes include boiled eggs served with a thick curry sauce and egg pie (garnished with a little minced meat and salad). You can also try a rare dish of eggs removed from the hen before they're laid. Ask for *mayai mabichi tumboni*.

EATING OUT

Cheese

Not much cheese is produced in East Africa, so cheese dishes aren't very popular. However, that of the Kenyan highlands is particularly well known.

jibini ya kupakaa	cheese spread
kimanda cha jibini	cheese omelet
kiungo cha mkate na gii cha safari	"Safari" cheese sandwich (submarine sandwich)
ladu ya jibini	sweet cheese ball
tosti ya jibini	toasted cheese

Soups

As one might expect, soup isn't common in such hot countries as those in East Africa. The variety is limited, too. Of course, in most large hotels—at least those in principal cities and coastal resorts—you can usually ask for your favourite Western soup.

Do you have ...?	**Unayo ...?**
I'd like some ...	**Nitapenda ...**
barley soup	mchuzi wa ngano
consommé	konsome
cream of chicken soup	mchuzi mzito wa kuku
cream of tomato soup	mchuzi wa nyanya
green pea soup	mchuzi wa pojo
potato soup	mchuzi wa viazi vya mviringo
pumpkin soup	mchuzi wa malenge
cream of rice soup	mchuzi wa wali

East African soups

mchuzi mwepesi wa mboga	vegetable soup
mchuzi mwepesi wa ngombe	consommé
mchuzi mzito wa ngano ya kusagwa	semolina soup
mchuzi wa nazi	cream of coconut soup

Fish and seafood

Fish is naturally plentiful in coastal regions while it may not even be known in some hinterland areas. However, you can get freshwater fish around Lake Victoria and other large lakes. Also, why not try one of the local seafood specialities listed on page 48?

I'd like some fish.	**Ningetaka samaki.**
What kind of seafood do you have?	**Mna aina gani ya chakula cha baharini?**

aina ya kaa	crayfish
changu	white mackerel
chaza	oysters
dagaa	sardines
kaa	crab
kamba	lobster
kamba kamba	shrimp
mkizi	cod
mkunga	eel
mkunga wa kukaushwa	smoked eel
nguru	salmon
nguru wa kukaushwa	smoked salmon
papa	trout
perege	herring
peshi	perch
samoni	salmon
samoni wa kukaushwa	smoked salmon
sumbururu	tunny (tuna)
tasi	herring
tilapia	a local salt-water fish

There are many ways of preparing fish.

baked	**aliyepalizwa**
barbecued	**aliyechomwa kwa makaa**
fried	**aliyekaangwa**
deep fried	**aliyekaangwa mafutani**
grilled	**aliyechomwa**
poached	**aliyechemshwa**
raw	**mbichi**
smoked	**aliyekaushwa**
steamed	**aliyepikwa kwa mvuke**
stewed	**aliyetokoswa**

You can also have it prepared with different ingredients:

bia [pombe]	beer
mayai	eggs
maziwa	milk
siki	vinegar
unga	flour

Fish and seafood specialities

aina ya kaa wa kuchemshwa	local speciality of crayfish or lobster
kaa wa kuchemshwa	crab plate with local seasoning
kamba wa kukaanga mafutani	deep-fried prawns
mkunga wa kukaanga	deep-fried eel
papa mbichi	sun-dried trout, marinated and served with lemon, raw onions and tomatoes
samaki wa chukuchuku	boiled fish, dressed with a curry sauce and served with rice
samaki wa kukaanga	fried fish, served with chips (french fries) or crisps (potato chips) and pickled vegetables
samaki wa kukausha	baked fish, usually served with pancakes
samaki wa kupaka	a typical coastal dish. Baked fish flavoured with coconut milk and spices. A delicious meal with *chapati* or *mkate wa tanuri* (pancakes).
tilapia wa kukaangwa mafutani	deep-fried *tilapia*

EATING OUT

Meat

The inland part of East Africa is known for its cattle raising and hence has good beef. You can order pork in major cities but areas with a predominantly Moslem population won't offer it due to religious reasons. Lamb is popular in the northern part of Kenya as well as throughout Uganda and certain parts of Tanzania.

What kind of meat do you have?	**Aina gani ya nyama unayo?**
I'd like some …	**Nataka …**
beef	**nyama ya ng'ombe**
lamb/mutton	**nyama ya kondoo**
pork	**nyama ya nguruwe**
veal	**nyama ya ndama**

kipande cha kondoo	lamb chops
kondoo	lamb
mafigo	kidneys
maini	liver
mbuzi	goat
mguu wa kondoo	leg of lamb
ndama	veal
ndama aliyesagwa	veal sausage
ng'ombe	beef
ng'ombe aliyesagwa	beef sausage
nguruwe aliyesagwa	pork sausage
nyama ya kuponda	minced meat
nguruwe	pork
paja la kondoo	breast of lamb
paja la nguruwe	ham
soseji	sausages
steki	steak (in general)
steki ya mbuzi	goat steak
steki ya ng'ombe	beefsteak
sungura	hare
ubongo	brains
ulimi	tongue

EATING OUT

How do you like your meat?

baked	iliyookwa
barbecued	iliyochomwa kwa makaa
boiled	iliyochemshwa
braised	iliyopashwa
fried	iliyokaangwa
grilled	iliyochomwa
roasted	iliyokaushwa
stewed	mchuzi wa ...
stuffed	iliyojazwa
medium	ya kuiva kiasi
rare	iliyoiva kidogo
well-done	iliyoiva sawa sawa

East African meat dishes

kababu	meat balls
katlesi ya ng'ombe	beef fillet covered with hashed brown potatoes
kima iliyokaangwa	fried minced meat
matumbo	tripe with seasonings
mchuzi wa kima	curried minced meat
mchuzi wa kondoo	lamb curry
mchuzi wa mbuzi	goat curry
mshakiki wa maini	skewer-grilled liver
ndama aliyechomwa	roast veal
ng'ombe aliyechomwa	roast beef
nyama ya kuponda	minced meat
soseji na mkate wa tanuri	sausage wrapped in a pancake

In addition to this, you can also get bacon *(nyama ya nguruwe iliyohifadhiwa),* cold meat *(nyama iliyohifadhiwa kwa barafu)* or ham *(nyama ya nguruwe)* at most hotel restaurants in major cities.

EATING OUT

Game and fowl

You'll doubtless want to sample some of the exotic game listed on page 89. But don't forget that such plates won't be available in the westernized restaurants on the coast and in major cities, where, on the other hand, you'll be able to dine on the more usual dishes of game and fowl.

I'd like some game/fowl.	**Ninataka nyama ya mwituni/ kanga.**

bata	duck
bata mchanga	duckling
bata mzinga	goose
bata mzinga wa kukausha	roast goose
bata wa kukaanga	fried duck
bata wa kukausha	roast duck
dikidiki	dik-dik (kind of antelope)
kanga	guinea fowl
kongoni	hartebeest (kind of antelope)
kuku	stewing hen
kuku mdogo	chicken
kuru	waterbuck (kind of antelope)
maini ya kuku	chicken liver
mayai ya bata	duck eggs
mbuni	pheasant
mguu wa kuku	chicken leg
mguu wa paa	leg of venison
ndege wa pwani	sea gull
nguruwe dume	wild boar
njiwa	pigeon
nyati	buffalo
paa	venison
pavu la paa	venison tenderloin
pofu	antelope
pugi	a kind of dove
sungura wa mjini	rabbit
sungura wa pori	hare
swala	impala (kind of antelope)
tandala mkubwa	kudu (kind of antelope)

EATING OUT

Game and fowl dishes

Due to Indian influence, East Africa is renowned for its curry specialities, e.g., chicken curry *(mchuzi wa kuku)*, which is normally prepared with carrots, onions and tomatoes. Genuine curry comprises no less than seventy different spices.

biriani ya kuku	delicately prepared rice with chicken
katlesi ya kuku	breast of chicken covered with hashed brown potatoes
kuku na mayai yake	roast chicken stuffed with eggs
kuku aliyejazwa	baked chicken stuffed with rice
kuku aliyepakwa	roast chicken with a gravy of coconut milk. Try it with *mkate wa tanuri* (baked pancakes).
mchuzi wa kuku	chicken curry
njiwa aliyekaangwa	fried pigeon
njiwa aliyekaushwa	roast chicken; served as an appetizer
paa aliyekaangwa	fried venison steaks
pilau ya kuku	spicy fried rice with chicken

Vegetables and seasonings

What vegetables do you have?

Una mboga gani?

I prefer some salad.

Napenda saladi.

aina ya mzizi	turnips
bamia	lady's fingers, vetch
biringani	aubergine (eggplant)
bitiruti	beetroot
choroko	lentils
dengu	peas
dodoki	pumpkin
figili	lettuce
fiwi	butter beans
hadesi	red lentils
kabeji	cabbage
karoti	carrots
kaulifulawa	cauliflower
kiukamba ya tango	gherkins (pickles)
kunde	white beans
liiki	leeks
maharagwe	haricot beans (green beans)
mahindi	corn
majimbi	sweet potatoes, yams
mbaazi	peas
mbaazi mbichi	green peas
mbatata vya Kizungu	potatoes
mboga	spinach
mhogo	cassava
mtama	millet
mumunye	marrow (zucchini)
nyanya	tomatoes
nyanya za mshumaa	green tomatoes
pesili	parsley
seleri	celery
tango	cucumber
tungule	cherry tomatoes
uyoga	mushrooms
viazi vya Kiingereza	potatoes
viazi vitamu	sweet potatoes
viazi vyekundu	radishes
vitunguu	onions
wali	rice
wanga	arrowroot

EATING OUT

Vegetable dishes

The most popular vegetables are beans (several varieties) and sweet potatoes. But meat dishes are often served with cassava, coconut flesh or milk, sorghum (a kind of millet) or bananas. Rice—with or without meat, but with curry or vegetables—is also very common, because of the Indian influence. A frequent side-dish is semolina (*ugali* or *sima*), especially in Tanzania. It's prepared in such a way that the cook is able to gather a ball of it in his hand, make a hole inside and serve it with a broth or a sauce; sometimes, it's also sliced like cake. Plantains are another fruit served as a side-dish; these are related to the "sweet" bananas that we know, but are used green and cooked as a vegetable. Their taste resembles that of mashed potatoes.

chipsi za mhogo	cassava chips
dodoki la sukari	pumpkin cooked in coconut milk
tango ya papa	dried fish, cucumbers and pickles
kachori ya samaki [nyama]	cassava dumplings with fish or meat
makopa ya tangawizi	sun-dried cassava cooked with ginger
matoke na achari	cooked green bananas and pickles
matoke na matumbo ya mbuzi	green bananas cooked with lamb tripe
mboga ya kisambo [mayugwa]	cassava leaves mixed with tomatoes and cooked in yoghurt
mhogo wa kuchoma na nanaa	fried cassava with mint
mseto na samaki	mixed rice and lentils with fish
sambusa ya vitunguu	onion pie, samosas

ugali [sima] na mtoriro	cassava and maize (corn) meal with yam (sweet-potato) leaves
viazi vya kuchemshwa kwa nyanya na nanaa	boiled potatoes with tomatoes and mint

Condiments and spices

Remember that East Africa is well-known for its spices. Zanzibar is even the first producer of cloves in the world. But different kinds of pepper and curry are also used—quite generously.

With cold plates, but sometimes also with other dishes, a selection of pickled vegetables and spices are provided—to which you help yourself. However, before heaping them joyfully onto your plate you'd better take just a tiny sample of each first, to make sure they aren't too hot for you … and don't overestimate your possibilities. Mango, lemon, paprika with lemon slices in vinegar, Indian spices (curry, Cayenne pepper, cardimome, dried pepper), cloves, are all known under the generic name of *viungo*.

achari	mixed pickles
chatne ya embe	grated coconut and sour-mango chutney
chatne ya karoti na ndimu	carrot and lemon chutney
haradali	strong local mustard
karafuu	cloves
mastadi	mustard
mchuzi	curry
pilipili	pepper
pilipili isiyokaki	black pepper
pilipili kali	chili pepper
pilipili siyoiva	green pepper
siki	vinegar
thomu	garlic
zafarani	saffron
zeituni	olives

EATING OUT

Fruit

Do you have fresh fruit?	**Unayo matunda freshi?**
I'd like very ripe ones.	**Nataka yaliyoiva sana.**
Not too ripe, please.	**Yasiyoiva sana, tafadhali.**
I'd like some sugar, please.	**Nataka sukari pamoja na tunda.**

aprikoti	apricots
avokado	avocado
blek beri	blackberries
boga	pumpkin
chenza	tangerines
chungwa	orange
danzi	grapefruit
embe	mango
embe za boribo	large mangoes
embe za kufyonza	small sweet mangoes
fenesi	jack-fruit (kind of melon)
korosho	cashews
lozi	almonds
mabibo	apricots
mapera	guavas
matofaa	apples
muwa	sugar cane
mzuzu	plantains (type of banana)
nanasi	pineapple
nazi	coconut
ndimu	lemon
ndimu tamu	sweet lemon
ndizi	bananas
njugu karanga	groundnuts
njugu nyasa	peanuts
papai	paw paw, papaw
peya	pear
plam	plums
sheli sheli	bread-fruit
strawberi	strawberries
tende	dates
tikitiki	watermelon
tini	figs
zabibu mbichi	grapes
zabibu nyekundu	sultanas
zabibu nyeusi	raisins
zambarau	velvet plums

Also try some of the following fruit:

dafu	unripe coconut sold in the streets on the coast, its sweet juice is refreshing in the hot climate. you can also eat its thin fleshy part.
shoki shoki	small fruit with red chunky skin; eat the flesh inside and throw away the pit.
stafeli	mango-shaped fruit with hard skin; sweet with plenty of seeds inside .

Dessert

If you've survived all the courses on the menu, you may want to say:

I'd like a dessert, please.	**Tafadhali ningependa chakula cha mwisho.**
Something light, please.	**Kitu chepesi tafadhali.**
Just a small portion.	**Kiasi kidogo tu.**
Nothing more, thanks.	**Imetosha, asante.**

If you aren't sure what to order, ask the waiter:

I'd like a/an ...	**Nataka ...**
apple pie	**keki ya tunda**
fruit in syrup	**tunda ndani ya asali**
fruit in syrup laced with liquor	**tunda ndani ya asali na speriti**
ice-cream	**barafu ya kirimu**

In addition to Western desserts served in hotel restaurants you can ask for local specialities. Some Asian restaurants serve delicious desserts.

EATING OUT

What do you have for dessert?	**Una kitu gani kwa chakula cha mwisho?**
What do you recommend?	**Unapendekeza kitu gani?**
faluda	jelly; the local type is made of milk or water, jelly leaves and cardamom or rose essence.
farne	ground rice with milk
haluwa	sweetmeat, similar to Turkish delight; take it with local coffee.
kaimati	Swahili version of doughnuts; these are small balls served plain or soaked in syrup.
kitumbua	oily cakes made of rice flour and toddy (palm sap)
ndizi tamu za kupika	sweet bananas cooked with coconut milk; the best type are the large ones called *mkono wa tembo* (elephant's leg)
ndizi za kukaanga	fried plantains; special type of banana which can be fried when they're too ripe
pudini	caramel pudding
pudini ya mchele	rice pudding served either with sugar or jam

The bill (check)

I'd like to pay.	**Nataka kulipa.**
May I please have the bill (check)?	**Unaweza kunipa jumla ya hesabu?**
We'd like to pay separately.	**Fanya hesabu kila mtu pekee.**
You made a mistake in this bill, I think.	**Nafikiri umefanya makosa katika hesabu hii.**
What is this amount for?	**Jumla hii ni ya kitu gani?**
Is service included?	**Je, ni pamoja na malipo ya utumishi?**
Is the cover charge included?	**Pamoja na malipo ya mwanzo?**
Is everything included?	**Hiyo ni jumla vyote?**
Do you accept traveller's cheques?	**Utakubali malipo kwa hawala ya safari?**
Thank you, this is for you.	**Asante, na hii kwa ajili yako.**
Keep the change.	**Chukua hizo zilobakia.**
That was a very good meal.	**Chakula hicho kilikwa kizuri sana.**
We enjoyed it, thank you.	**Tumefurahi, asante.**

> **PAMOJA NA UTUMISHI**
> SERVICE INCLUDED

EATING OUT

Complaints

But perhaps you'll have something to complain about:

That's not what I ordered. I asked for ...	**Hicho sicho nilichoagiza. Niliomba nipatiwe ...**
May I change this?	**Naweza kubadilisha hii?**

The meat is ...	Nyama hii ...
overdone	imepikwa sana
underdone	imepikwa kidogo
too rare	haijapikwa sana
too tough	ngumu sana
This is too ...	Hii ni ... sana.
bitter/salty/sweet	kakasi/chungu/tamu mno
The food is cold.	Chakula kimepoa.
This isn't fresh.	Hii si safi.
What's taking you so long?	Nini kinachokuweka muda huu?
Where are our drinks?	Vipo wapi vinywaji vyetu?
This isn't clean.	Hii si safi.
Would you ask the head waiter to come over?	Unaweza kumwita msimamizi wa utumishi aje hapa?

EATING OUT

Drinks

Beer

Don't forget to try the locally-brewed beer, made of millet, maize or banana *(moshi)*.

local beer	bia [pombe] ya kienyeji
imported beer	bia [pombe] ya nje
light beer	bia [pombe] nyepesi
non-alcoholic beer	bia [pombe] isiyo ya kulevya
palm-tree beer	bia [pombe] ya mnazi
I'd like a (cold) beer, please.	Tafadhali nataka bia [pombe] (baridi).
I'd like a glass of moshi, please.	Nitapenda kujaribu bilauri ya moshi.

Wine

All wines are imported and they're relatively expensive, except for some foreign brands of vermouth which are locally produced. While eating, East Africans prefer beer or local spirits to wine.

I want a bottle of white/red wine.	**Nataka chupa ya divai nyeupe/ nyekundu.**
I don't want anything too sweet.	**Sitaki kitu chochote kilicho kitamu mno.**
How much is a bottle of ...?	**Kima [Kiasi] gani chupa ya ...?**
That's too expensive.	**Hiyo ni ghali sana.**
Haven't you anything cheaper?	**Huna kitu kingine kilicho rahisi?**
Fine, that'll do.	**Vizuri, hiyo itafaa.**

If you enjoyed the wine, you may want to say:

Please bring me another ...	**Tafadhali niletee ... zaidi.**
glass/carafe/bottle	**bilauri/jagi/chupa**
What's this wine called?	**Divai hii inaitwaje?**
Where does this wine come from?	**Divai hii imetoka wapi?**
How old is this wine?	**Divai hii ina miaka mingapi?**

dry	kavu
red	nyekundu
rosé	waridi
sparkling	enye kung'aa
sweet	tamu
white	nyeupe
chilled	iliyofaniwa baridi
at room temperature	katika hewa ya chumbani

EATING OUT

Local alcoholic beverages

Locally produced alcohols are not common in all parts of East Africa, as there is an important proportion of Moslems. Also, the consumption of certains drinks, such as *chang'aa* (usually made from the fruit of the loofah plant), *kanga* (distilled from local grain and/or vegetables) and *mutukuru* (distilled from maize or wheat) has been lately prohibited by the Kenyan Government, because of their high alcoholic content.

However, there are a few national specialities, like *Kenya Cane* (resembling rum), *Konyagi* (a kind of Tanzanian brandy) and *Waragi* (Uganda). But be careful, as they may be very strong. If you happen to be in an area where bananas form part of the staple diet, ask for the local variety of banana brandy *(pombe mandizi)*.

Are there any local specialities?	**Je, kipo kinywaji cha hapa kwenu?**
Please bring me a bottle of toddy.	**Tafadhali niletee chupa ya tembo.**

buzaa (kanga)	nubian gin
tembo	literally "elephant": palm-tree toddy, often very hot, due to the spices which are added to it
tende	strong, fermented drink, the composition of which may vary from region to region

glass	**bilauri**
bottle	**chupa**
single (shot)	**pegi moja**
double (double shot)	**pegi mbili**

CHEERS [KARIBU, TUNYWE]
CHEERS!

EATING OUT

Other beverages

Try *sharubati* (milk-coloured sherbet with herbs) or *maziwa ya lozi* (fresh milk with almonds). In some areas, especially in coastal regions, you may be able to get *maji ya maembe* (mango juice).

I'd like a/an/some ...	Nataka ...
Have you any ...?	Unayo ...?
chocolate	chakleti
coffee	kahawa
cup of coffee	kikombe cha kahawa
coffee with cream	kahawa na maziwa mtindi
espresso coffee	kahawa ya espresso
iced coffee	kahawa ya barafu
fruit juice	maji ya matunda
grapefruit	maji ya mabalungi
lemon/orange	maji ya ndimu/machungwa
pineapple/tomato	maji ya nanasi/nyanya
lemonade	soda ya ndimu
milk	maziwa
milkshake	milkshake
orangeade	soda ya machungwa
soda water	maji safi ya soda
squash (fruit drink)	squash
tea	chai
with milk/lemon	na maziwa/ndimu
iced tea	chai baridi
tonic water	maji ya tonik

Except in the larger towns mineral water is rarely available.

Eating light—Snacks

East Africa abounds in open-air snack-bars or stands, and some cities boast the occasional restaurant *(kula kidogo)* catering specifically to the needs of the hurried passer-by in search of light refreshment. Try a roll with *mshikati* (pieces of meat roasted on a skewer).

I'll have on of those, please.	**Tafadhali nipe ile moja.**
to the left/right	**kushoto/kulia**
Give me a/an/some ...	**Nipe ...**
biscuits (cookies)	**biskuti**
bread	**mkate**
brown bread	**mkate wa ngano nzima**
butter	**siagi**
cake	**keki**
candy	**peremende [vitu vya utami]**
canned beef	**nyama ya ng'ombe ya mkebeni**
cheese	**jibini**
chocolate bar	**kipande cha chakleti**
hamburger	**hambaga**
ham	**nyama ya nguruwe**
herring	**samaki wa ulaya**
hot dog	**kitumbua cha nyama**
ice-cream	**sikirimu**
lemon	**ndimu**
pastry	**kinyunya**
pie	**andazi**
roll	**kipande cha bofulo**
salad	**saladi**
salt	**chumvi**
sandwich	**sendwichi**
with cheese	**ya jibini**
with ham	**ya nyama**
sardines	**samaki wadogo kama simsim**
small cakes	**mikati ya tamu midogo**
sugar	**sukari**
sweets	**peremende [vitu vya utami]**
toast	**tosti**
How much is that?	**Kima [Kiasi] gani ile?**

EATING OUT

Travelling around

Plane

Very brief—because at any airport you're sure to find someone who speaks English.

In order to cover some of the vast distances in East Africa, you'll doubtless find it practical to fly. You'll save money by buying a return (roundtrip) ticket. During holidays watch for special excursion fares which often represent a considerable savings over ordinary ticket prices.

Besides the commercial airlines serving East African cities, air-taxi service is available. For such chartered aircraft, fares are calculated both per mile and per passenger for usually three-seat Cessna planes.

Here are a few useful expressions you may want to know …

Do you speak English?	**Unasema Kiingereza?**
Is there a flight to Mombasa?	**Ipo ndege kwenda Mombasa?**
Is it a nonstop flight?	**Ndege isiyotua safarini?**
When's the next plane to Zanzibar?	**Wakati gani ndege ijayo yaenda Zanzibar?**
Do I have to change planes?	**Itabidi nibadilishe ndege?**
Can I make a connection to Entebbe?	**Eti yawezekana kuunganisha safari kwenda Entebbe?**
I'd like a ticket to Kampala.	**Nataka tikiti kwenda Kampala.**
What's the fare to Arusha?	**Kiasi gani kwenda Arusha?**
single (one-way)	**kwenda pekee**
return (roundtrip)	**kwenda na kurudi**

What time does the plane take off?	**Saa ngapi ndege itaruka?**
What time do I have to check in?	**Saa ngapi itabidi nifike kiwanjani?**
What's the flight number?	**Nambari ya ndege ni ngapi?**
What time do we arrive?	**Saa ngapi tutafika?**

```
KUWASILI
ARRIVAL
```

```
KUSAFIRI
DEPARTURE
```

Train and long distance bus

There are two principal railway lines in East Africa which link the coastal areas with the inland. These two lines are the Mombasa-Nairobi-Kampala-Kasese Line—1080 miles long—and the Dar es Salaam-Dodoma-Tabora-Kigoma which runs some 780 miles.

There are three classes on the trains. First class is very comfortable, second is adequate but don't expect more than wooden benches in third-class cars. Dining-*(gari la chakula)* and sleeping-cars *(gari la kulala)* are available.

Otherwise, railways are virtually non-existant in other parts of the region. To reach many towns and villages, the bus is the best means of public transportation—outside of taxis. Nearly always crowded, buses offer a very cheap mode of transportation.

A number of taxi companies have organized a taxi network serving outlying regions in the vicinity of towns. They run regularly along certain routes, and you can reserve a seat in advance. Generally, they aren't very expensive although their set fares can be six times higher than that of buses. The fare for urban taxis is per mile.

It might be wise to hire a car though you'll have to be especially cautious driving over unfamiliar roads.

Phrases in this section can easily be adapted to either bus or train travel.

To the railway station

Where's the railway station?	**Wapi kituo cha gari la moshi?**
Where's the bus station?	**Stesheni ya basi iko wapi?**
Taxi, please!	**Nataka teksi.**
Take me to the railway station.	**Nipeleke kituo cha gari la moshi.**
Take me to the bus station.	**Nipeleke kituo cha mabasi.**

KUINGIA	ENTRANCE
KUTOKA	EXIT
KWA JUKWAA	TO THE PLATFORMS

Where's the ... ?	**Ipo wapi ... ?**
Where is/are the ... ?	**Ipo wapi/Yapo wapi ... ?**
bar	**pahali pa vinywaji**
barber's shop	**duka la kinyozi**
booking (reservations) office	**ofisi ya kufanyia safari**
buffet	**pahali pauzwapo chakula**
currency-exchange office	**ofisi ya kuvunja pesa**

information office	**ofisi ya maelezo**
left-luggage office (baggage check)	**ofisi ya kuweka mizigo**
lost-property (lost-and-found) office	**ofisi ya vitu vilivyopotea**
luggage lockers	**makabati ya kuweka mizigo**
news-stand	**muuzaji magazeti**
platform 4	**jukwaa nambari 4**
restaurant	**mkahawa**
ticket office	**pauzwapo tikiti**
waiting room	**pahali pa kusubiri**
Where's the telephone?	**Ipo wapi simu?**
Where are the toilets?	**Vipo wapi vyoo?**

TRAVELLING AROUND

HABARI ZA UTALII	TOURIST INFORMATION
KUVUNJA PESA	CURRENCY EXCHANGE

Inquiries

TOURIST INFORMATION is always written out in English in Kenya, Uganda and Tanzania.

When is the ... train to Tsavo?	**Wakati gani gari la moshi ... laenda Tsavo?**
first/last/next	**ya kwanza/ya mwisho/ijayo**
What time does the train for Nyeri leave?	**Saa ngapi litaondoka gari la moshi kwenda Nyeri?**
What's the fare to Moshi?	**Nauli ni kiasi gani kwenda Moshi?**
Is it a through train?	**Ni gari la moshi liendalo mbio?**
Will the train leave on time?	**Eti gari la moshi litaondoka kwa kawaida?**

What time does the train arrive at Nairobi?	**Saa ngapi gari la moshi litafika Nairobi?**
Is there a dining-car on the train?	**Upo mkahawa ndani ya gari la moshi?**
Is there a sleeping-car on the train?	**Kipo chumba cha kulala ndani ya gari la moshi?**
Does the train stop at Voi?	**Gari la moshi litasimama Voi?**
What platform does the train for Tabora leave from?	**Jukwaa gani lipo gari la moshi liendalo Tabora?**
What platform does the train from ... arrive at?	**Jukwaa gani litafika gari la moshi kutoka ... ?**

Ni gari la moshi liendalo mbio.	It's a through train.
Itabidi ubadilishe ukifika ...	You have to change at ...
Jukwaa nambari ... ipo ...	Platform ... is ...
pale	over there
upande kushoto	on the left
upande kulia	on the right
Lipo gari la moshi liendalo ... saa ...	There's a train to ... at ...
Gari la moshi lako litaondoka kutoka jukwaa nambari ...	Your train will leave from platform ...
Litachelewa kwa muda wa dakika ...	There'll be a delay of ... minutes.

TRAVELLING AROUND

Tickets

I want a ticket to Jinja.	**Nataka tikiti kwenda Jinja.**
single (one-way)	**kwenda pekee**
return (roundtrip)	**kwenda na kurudi**
first class	**daraja ya kwanza**
Isn't it half-price for the boy/girl?	**Eti si nusu ya nauli kwa mtoto.**
He's/She's 13.	**Ana umri wa miaka 13.**

Daraja ya kwanza au ya pili?	First or second class?
Kwenda pekee au kwenda na kurudi?	Single or return (one-way or roundtrip)?
Ana umri gani?	How old is he/she?

All aboard

Excuse me. May I get past?	**Tafadhali, ebu nipite.**
Is this seat taken?	**Kiti hiki kimechukuliwa?**
Is this seat free?	**Kiti hiki kiko wazi?**
I think that's my seat.	**Ninafikiri kile ndicho kiti changu.**

USIVUTE SIGARA
NO SMOKING

TRAVELLING AROUND

Can you tell me when we get to Nairobi?	**Unaweza kuniambia tutafika lini (kule) Nairobi?**
What station is this?	**Tuko kishecheni kipi?**
How long does the train stop here?	**Gari la moshi litasimama hapa kwa muda gani?**
When do we get to Mombasa?	**Tutafika Mombasa lini?**

Some time on the journey the ticket-collector *(mkusanya ji wa tikiti)* will come around and say:

| Tickets, please! | **Tafadhali nionyeshe tikiti!** |

Eating

There's usually a dining-car on long-distance trains where you can get meals and drinks. On many trains, depending on the class, an attendant comes around with snacks, biscuits and soft drinks.

| First/Second call for dinner. | **Uwito wa kwanza/Pili kwa chakula.** |
| Where's the dining-car? | **Upo wapi mkahawa?** |

Sleeping

Are there any free compartments in the sleeping-car?	**Ipo nafasi tupu katika kijumba cha kulala?**
Where's the sleeping-car?	**Kiko wapi kijumba cha kulala?**
Where's my berth?	**Kipo wapi kitanda changu?**
Compartments 18 and 19, please.	**Nataka kijumba nambari 18 na 19, tafadhali.**
I'd like a lower berth.	**Napenda kitanda cha chini.**

Would you make up our berths?	**Unaweza kuweka sawa vitanda vyetu?**
Would you call me at 7 o'clock?	**Unaweza kuniamsha saa 7 asubuhi?**
Would you bring me some coffee in the morning?	**Unaweza kuniletea kahawa asubuhi?**

Baggage and porters

Can you help me with my bags?	**Unaweza kunisaidia na mizigo yangu?**
Please put them down here.	**Tafadhali iweke hapa.**

Note: If you want to have your baggage put into the guard's van (baggage car—*gari la mzi*), you'd better register it in advance.

Time-tables

If you intend to do a lot of rail travel, it might be a good idea to buy a time-table. These are based on the 24-hour clock and are on sale at ticket and inquiry offices and at travel agencies. Time-tables giving both rail and air connections for the whole of East Africa are available for tourists.

I'd like to buy a time-table.	**Nataka kununua orodha ya wakati wa gari la moshi.**

SIMAMA BASI KWA KAWAIDA	REGULAR BUS STOP
SIMAMA KWA MAHITAJI TU	STOPS ON REQUEST

FOR PORTERS, see also page 24

Bus

You can buy your ticket on the bus from the conductor.
Just mention your destination and he'll tell you the fare.

There are no season tickets in East Africa; for long trips,
most bus companies require that you buy your ticket in
advance in order to reserve you a seat.

Where can I get a bus to the university?	Wapi nitapata basi kwenda chuo kikuu?
What bus do I take for the parliament square?	Basi gani nichukue kwenda mahali pa bunge?
Where's the ... ?	Ipo wapi ...?
bus station	stesheni ya basi
bus stop	kituo cha basi
terminus	mahali pa safari za bara
When is the ... bus to Machakos?	Wakati gani basi ya ... inakwenda Machakos?
first/last/next	kwanza/mwisho/ijayo
How often do the buses go to Bagamoyo?	Kwa kawaida gani basi huenda Bagamoyo?
How much is the fare ...?	Nauli ni kiasi gani kwenda ...?
Do I have to change buses?	Itabidi nibadilishe mabasi?
How long does the journey take?	Safari itachukua muda gani?
Will you tell me when to get off?	Unaweza kuniarifu mahali ambapo nitateremka?
I want to get off at the Aga Khan mosque.	Nataka kuteremka kwenye msikiti wa Aga Khan.
Please let me off at the next stop.	Tafadhali niteremshe kwenye kituo kinachofuata.
May I please have my luggage?	Unaweza kunipa mizigo yangu?

Other means of transportation

A slightly off-beat, and sometimes really idyllic, way of travelling between the islands is by *dhow* (large sailing-boat typical of this part of Africa). However, the three East African countries are served by regular coastal and lake shipping service. Ask a travel agent for steamer schedules.

The locals prefer donkeys for short distances. They won't mind your climbing on for a ride if you express your appreciation in the form of a modest tip.

Or try one of these to get around:

bicycle	**baiskeli**
boat	**mashua**
houseboat	**ngalawa**
motorboat	**mashua ya injini**
rowing-boat	**mashua ya kasia**
sailing-boat	**mashua ya tanga**
helicopter	**helikopta**
hitch-hiking	**kupakiwa-njiani**
horseback riding	**kupanda farasi**
moped	**baiskeli ya moto**
motorcycle (motor-bike)	**pikipiki**

and if you're really stuck, start ...

walking	**nenda kwa miguu**

Lost

We hope you'll have no need for the following phrases on your trip... but just in case:

Where's the lost-property (lost-and-found) office?	**Ipo wapi ofisi ya vitu viliopotea?**
I've lost my ...	**Nimepoteza ... yangu.**
this morning	**leo asubuhi**
yesterday	**jana**
I lost it in ...	**Nimepoteza katika ...**
It's very valuable.	**Ina thamani kubwa.**

Around and about—Sightseeing

Here we're more concerned with the cultural aspect of life than with entertainment and, for the moment, with towns rather than the countryside. If you want a guide book, ask ...

Can you recommend a good guide book for ...?	**Unaweza kunisifia buku zuri la maelezo ya utalii ya ...?**
Is there a tourist office?	**Iko ofisi ya habari za utalii?**
Where's the tourist office/information centre?	**Iko wapi ofisi ya habari za utalii/mahali pa habari?**
What are the main points of interest?	**Mahali gani pasifika kwa matembezi?**
We're here for ...	**Tupo hapa kwa ...**
only a few hours	**saa chache tu**
a day	**siku moja**
three days	**siku tatu**
a week	**wiki moja**
Can you recommend a sightseeing tour?	**Unaweza kunisifia u ongozi wa utalii?**
Where does the bus start from?	**Basi litaondoka kutoka wapi?**
Will it pick us up at the hotel?	**Litapita kutuchukua kutoka hoteli?**
What bus do we take?	**Tuchukue basi gani?**
How much does the tour cost?	**Kiasi gani gharama ya matembezi?**
What time does the tour start?	**Matembezi yataanza saa ngapi?**

FOR TIME OF DAY, see page 177

SIGHTSEEING

We'd like to rent a car for the day.	**Tungapenda kukodi gari kwa siku moja.**
Is there an English-speaking guide?	**Yuko mwonyeshaji wa utalii anayesma Kiingereza?**
Where is/Where are the ...?	**Iko wapi/Ziko wapi...?**
aquarium	**tangi la kuwekea samaki**
art gallery	**nyumba ya sanaa**
botanical gardens	**bustani ya maua**
business district	**mtaa wa biashara**
castle	**ngome**
catacombs	**pango la mazishi**
cathedral	**kanisa kuu**
cave	**pango**
cemetery	**mkaburi**
cinema	**senema**
city centre	**kati ya mji**
city hall	**ukumbi wa mji**
church	**kanisa**
community house	**nyumba ya jamii**
concert hall	**ukumbi wa tarabu**
court house	**nyumba ya mahakama [korti]**
docks	**forodha [gati]**
downtown area	**mjini**
exhibition	**maonyesho**
factory	**kiwanda [karakana]**
football field	**uwanja wa mpira**
fortress	**boma**
fountain	**chemchemi**
gardens	**bustani [shamba]**
harbour	**bandari**
lake	**ziwa la maji**
market	**soko**
memorial	**ukumbusho**
monument	**ukumbusho**
mosque	**msikiti [jamati]**
museum	**makumbusho**
opera house	**nyumba ya michezo**
palace	**jumba la sifa**
park	**bustani ya starehe**
parliament building	**nyumba ya bunge**
pottery	**mahali pa kufinyanga**
presidential palace	**jumba la rais [Ikulu]**

radio station	nyumba ya radio
royal palace	jumba la mfalme
ruins	gofu la nyumba
shopping centre	mahali pa maduka
stadium	uwanja wa michezo
statue	sanamu
synagogue	hekalu la kiyahudi
temple	hekalu
tomb	kaburi
tower	mnara
university	chuo kikuu
zoo	zizi la wanyama wa porini

People usually don't mind if you take their picture, but it's best to ask first and give them a small tip afterwards.

Admission

Is ... open on Sundays?	...yafunguliwa Jumapili?
When does it open/close?	Wakati gani yafunguliwa/yafungwa?
How much is the entrance fee?	Kiasi gani ada ya kuingia?
Is there any reduction for ...?	Iko nakisi kwa ...?
students/children	wanafunzi/watoto
Here's my ticket.	Hii ni tikiti yangu.
Have you a guide book in English?	Unacho kitabu cha uongozi kwa Kiingereza?
Can I buy a catalogue?	Yawezekana kununua katalogi?
Is it all right to take pictures?	Utaniruhusu nipige picha?

| KUINGIA BURE | ADMISSION FREE |
| USICHUKUE PICHA | NO CAMERAS ALLOWED |

SIGHTSEEING

Who—What—When?

What's that building?	**Lile jumba gani?**
Who was the ...?	**Nani ni ...?**
architect	**mjenzi**
artist	**mstadi**
painter	**mchoraji wa picha**
sculptor	**mchongaji wa mawe**
Who built it?	**Nani aliyeijenga?**
Who painted that picture?	**Nani aliyechora picha ile?**
When did he live?	**Mwaka gani aliishi?**
When was it built?	**Mwaka gani ilijengwa?**
We're interested in ...	**Sisi tunapenda ...**
Where's the ... department?	**Iko wapi idara ya ...?**
archaeology	**maarifa ya mambo ya kale**
art	**ustadi**
botany	**maarifa ya maua**
ceramics	**vyombo vya kauri**
coins	**sarafu**
crafts	**kazi za mkono**
furniture	**vifaa ya vifa nyumba**
geology	**maarifa ya mawe [udongo na ardhi]**
history	**historia**
medicine	**maarifa ya utabibu**
music	**muziki**
natural history	**historia ya maumbile**
ornithology	**maarifa ya ndege**
painting	**kuchora picha**
pottery	**vyombo vya udongo**
prehistory	**historia ya zama za kale**
sculpture	**kazi ya kuchora mawe**
wild life	**wanyama na ndege wa porini**
wood carving	**uchongaji**
zoology	**maarifa ya wanyama na ndege**

SIGHTSEEING

Just the adjective you've been looking for ...

It's ...	Ni ...
amazing	enye kushangaza
awful	enye kutisha
beautiful	ya kupendeza
interesting	enye kupendeza
overwhelming	ya ajabu
sinister	enye kisirani
strange	ya kigeni
superb	enye ukamilifu hasa
terrible	ya kuogofya
terrifying	ya kutisha
ugly	mnobaya

Religious services

Christianity claims roughly half the total population of East Africa. Adherents are divided about equally between Roman Catholic and Protestant faiths. Large communities of Moslems can be found in the coastal regions. In the mainland, the African traditional religion (ATR) is commonly practiced. Other major religions are represented in the cosmopolitan cities.

Services are conducted in English in many towns. Ask the local tourist office or check the Saturday newspapers for further details.

You'll be requested to take off your shoes before entering a mosque. Note that women are forbidden entry to certain parts of mosques.

Is there a ... near here?	Liko ... hapa karibu?
Catholic/Protestant/ Orthodox church	Kanisa la Kikatoliki/ Kiprotestanti/Kiorthodoxi
synagogue	hekalu la Kiyahudi
mosque	msikiti
At what time is ...?	Saa ngapi kuna ...?
mass/the service	sala ya misa/ibida

SIGHTSEEING

Relaxing

Cinema (movies)—Theatre

Cinemas in East Africa usually have three shows a day. The first showing normally starts around 3.30 p.m., the second at 6.30 p.m. and the third at 9.30 p.m. There may be a morning show during the weekend. Most of the films are in English, but there may be films in Swahili with English subtitles—or vice versa. Plays are rarely given, and they are mostly in English. Theatre curtain time is about 8 p.m. Advance booking is advisable.

You can expect one feature film, a newsreel, perhaps a short documentary and commercials. You can find out what's playing from newspapers and billboards.

Where can I find cinema programmes?	**Nitapata wapi habari za senema?**
What's showing at the cinema tonight?	**Picha gani itaonyeshwa kwenye senema leo jioni?**
What's playing at the ... Theatre?	**Kuna mchezo gani huko ... theatre?**
What sort of play is it?	**Mchezo wa namna gani huo?**
Who's it by?	**Nani aliyetunga mchezo?**
Can you recommend (a) ...?	**Unaweza kunisifia ...?**
good film	**picha ya senema nzuri**
comedy	**mchezo wa vichekesho**
something light	**mahali pa kupitisha wakati**
drama	**michezo ya hadithi**
musical	**tarabu**
revue	**mchezo wa ngoma**
thriller	**mchezo wa hofu**
Western	**mchezo wa kikaoboi wa kimarekani**

At what theatre are folk dances being performed?	**Mahali gani panachezewa ngoma na michezo ya kiasili?**
Where's that new film by... being shown?	**Mahali gani panaonyeshwa ile picha mpya ya ...?**
Who's in it?	**Nani wanaocheza?**
Who's playing the lead?	**Nani anayeongoza mchezo?**
Who's the director?	**Nani mkurugenzi wa mchezo?**
What time does it begin?	**Saa ngapi utaanza?**
What time does the show end?	**Saa ngapi utamalizika mchezo?**
What time does the first evening performance start?	**Saa ngapi utaanza mchezo wa kwanza wa usiku?**
Are there any tickets for tonight?	**Zipo tikiti kwa usiku wa leo?**
How much are the tickets?	**Bei [Kiasi] gani tikiti?**
I want to reserve two tickets for the show on Friday evening.	**Nataka kuagiza tikiti mbili za mchezo kwa usiku wa Ijumaa.**
Can I have a ticket for the matinée on Tuesday?	**Nataka tikiti ya mchezo wa alasiri kwa siku ya Jumanne.**
I want a seat in the stalls (orchestra).	**Nataka kiti kilichopo chini.**
Not too far back.	**Kisiwe pote nyuma sana.**
Somewhere in the middle.	**Popote pale kati kati.**
How much are the seats in the gallery (balcony)?	**Bei [Kiasi] gani tikiti ya roshani?**
May I please have a programme?	**Tafadhali nipe orodha ya mchezo.**
Where's the cloakroom?	**Kiko wapi choo?**

RELAXING

Samahani, hakuna tikiti.   I'm sorry, we're sold out.

Kuna viti vichache tu   There are only a few seats
vilivyobakia roshani.   left in the gallery (balcony).

Unaweza kuonyesha   May I see your ticket?
tikiti?

Hiki hapa kiti chako.   This is your seat.

Ballet—Concert

It would be presumptuous to expect operas and symphonic concerts in East Africa comparable to Western productions. However, there are cultural exchanges with most foreign countries, and performances are held either in the community centres or in spacious halls.

Is there any concert on this week?	**Kuna tarabu yoyote wiki hii?**
What orchestra is playing?	**Tarabu gani itacheza?**
What are they playing?	**Watacheza nini?**
Who's singing?	**Nani mwimbaji?**
Who's dancing?	**Nani mchezaji?**
What time does the programme start?	**Saa ngapi itaanza tarabu?**
How can I get there?	**Vipi nitafika mahali panapochezewa?**

RELAXING

Local dances

Few East African folk dances are tied to a particular setting. People are gay and lively and express their exuberance by singing and dancing in the streets. If you happen to be on the spot you can choose between being a spectator (free of charge) and a participant.

Gombe sugu	Comparable to what is danced in discotheques, this dance usually is performed outdoors. The movements are determined simply by the rhythm of the music.
Gombe sugu ya miti	A more sophisticated style of dancing: the performer shows off his talents by dancing with long sticks attached to his feet.
Tarabu ya asili	Women dressed in bright colours line up sidewise and swing from left to right to "cool" violin music.
Mwamvuli	An umbrella dance. Everyone who participates in this street processional must be carrying an opened umbrella. Raise it up and down in the air and march on. The band usually urges the dancers on from behind.

If your tastes lie in the direction of the more traditional dances why not take a trip to some of the rural villages at harvest time and watch the villagers dancing happily in celebration of their crop? They will be glad to let you sample their produce.

Pantomime

After a hard day's work the local people form a circle to enjoy a pantomime performance. The pantomimist is a purely lay artist who sometimes displays surprising talent and may exchange pranks with his audience. After watching this performance in the village park a modest tip (about two shillings) is considered as an appropriate sign of appreciation.

RELAXING

Night-clubs

Night-clubs (found, in East Africa, only in the major cities) are pretty much the same the world over—particularly when it comes to inflated prices. You can expect to pay a cover charge and your drinks will be expensive. The girls sitting around aren't there because they like the decor.

There are some reasonably-priced places that provide good entertainment, so ask around. But find out the prices before you order—and allow for the various surcharges.

Very few night-clubs ask for formal attire. In some cities a woman may be required to have an escort.

Can you recommend a good night-club?	Unaweza kunisifia klabu ya dansi iliyo nzuri?
Is there a floor show?	Kuna michezo maalum?
What time does the floor show start?	Saa ngapi utaanza mchezo maalum?
Is evening dress necessary?	Itabidi kuvaa suti ya usiku?
A table for two, please.	Tafadhali meza ya watu wawili.
My name's... I reserved a table for four.	Jina langu ni... Niliagiza meza ya watu wanne.
I telephoned you earlier.	Nilikupigia simu mapema.
We haven't got a reservation.	Hatukufanya agizo.

Dancing

Where can we go dancing?	Wapi tunaweza kwenda kucheza dansi?
Is there a discotheque in town?	Ipo discotheque hapa mjini?
May I have this dance?	Nifurahishe na dansi hii.

Do you happen to play?

On a rainy day, this page may solve your problems.

Do you happen to play chess?	Unapenda kucheza [chess] sataranji?
I'm afraid I don't.	Samahani sichezi.
No, but I'll give you a game of draughts (checkers).	Hapana, lakini maweza kucheza dama nawe.

king	mfalme
queen	malkia
rook (castle)	ngome
bishop	padri
knight	jamadari
pawn	kitunda

check mate	funga bao

Do you play cards?	Unacheza karata?

bridge	brijii [daraja]
canasta	kanasta

gin rummy	rami
whist	wist
pontoon (21)	ishirini na moja
poker	poka

ace	ree
king	mfalme [mzungu wa kwanza]
queen	malkia [mzungun wa pili]
jack	mzungu wa tatu
joker	joka

hearts	kopa
diamonds	uru [kashata]
clubs	pau
spades	shupaza

Or try some of the local card games ...

chanis	"calculation"
sitina na moja	sixty-one

On the beach

Most sea resorts offer beautiful, expansive beaches. As far as the inland is concerned, you should avoid bathing in rivers and lakes because of the possible danger of bilharziasis (a severe disease affecting the blood and tissue).

Is there a lifeguard?	Yupo askari wa kuokoa?
Is it safe for children?	Yafaa pia kwa watoto?
There are some big waves.	Kuna mawimbi makubwa.
Are there any dangerous currents?	Kuna mkondo wowote wa hatari?
What time is high tide?	Saa ngapi hujaa maji?
What time is low tide?	Saa ngapi maji hupwa?
What's the beach like— sandy or rocky?	Pwani ina hali gani— mchanga au mawe?
I want to hire (a/an) ...	Nataka kukodi ...
air mattress	godoro la upepo
bathing hut	kibanda cha pwani cha kuogelea
deck-chair	kiti cha pwani
skin-diving equipment	vyombo vya kupigia mbizi
sunshade	mwavuli wa pwani
surf board	ubao wa kusukumwa na mawimbi
tent	hema
some water-skis	wota-skis
Where can I hire (rent) a ...?	Wapi naweza kukodi ...?
canoe	mtumbwi
motor-boat	mashua ya injini
rowing-boat	mashua ya kasia
sailing-boat	mashua ya tanga
What's the charge per hour?	Kiasi gani cha kulipa [kukodi] kwa saa?

PWANI YA MTU PEKEE PRIVATE BEACH	**HAPANA KUOGELEA** NO BATHING

Sports

As far as spectator sports are concerned football
(soccer) is about as popular in East Africa as at home.
If you want to go on a horse-back riding holiday, it'd
be a good idea to book this in advance.

Where's the nearest golf course?	Wapi mahali karibu pa kucheza gofu?
Can we hire (rent) clubs?	Tunaweza kukodi virungu vya kuchezea gofu?
Where are the tennis courts?	Wapi mahali pa kucheza tufe [tennis]?
Can I hire rackets?	Naweza kukodi ubao wa kuchezea tufe [tennis]?
What's the charge per ...?	Nini gharama ya malipo nini kwa ...?
day/round/hour	siku/kila mchezo/saa
Where's the nearest race course (track)?	Wapi mahali karibu pa resi za farasi?
What's the admission charge?	Kiasi gani ada ya kuingia [kiingilio]?
Is there a swimming pool here?	Lipo bwawa [hapamu] la kuogelea hapa?
I'd like to see a boxing match.	Napenda kuangalia mchezo wa kupigana ngumi.
Can you get me a couple of tickets?	Unaweza kunipatia tikiti mbili?
Is there a football (soccer) match anywhere this Saturday?	Upo mchezo wa mpira mahali popote siku ya Jumamosi hii?
Who's playing?	Nani achezaye?

Mountaineering in this part of the world holds the
special attraction of the still untamed great outdoors. Surprising as it may seem, some people do go

to East Africa to ski, though facilities are limited to the Mount Kilimanjaro and Mount Kenya areas.

Can you recommend an interesting mountain to climb?	**Unaweza kunisifia mlima mzuri kwa kuparamia?**
Is there any snow?	**Kuna theluji huko?**
How can I go to Kilimanjaro?	**Vipi nitaweza kwenda Kilimanjaro?**

Photo safaris

Wildlife reservations are numerous in East Africa and photo safaris are very popular. They are organized into the bush in jeeps and minibuses with adjustable roofs to see the wildlife at close quarters. You will have many opportunities for photographing, filming and simple viewing with binoculars. Touring the parks and reserves is permitted only during daylight hours—roughly from 6 a.m. to 6 p.m.

For their own safety and to avoid disturbing the animals, tourists are confined to their vehicles during a safari, except at special signposted sites where it is permitted to walk about. The Ministry of Tourism and Wildlife will assign rangers to accompany you on game-runs and it is highly recommended that you make use of this service.

With so much arranged for you, don't be too upset if some animals don't choose to conform to the tour organizers' plans. You'll find a list of some of the animals with their Swahili names on the next page.

How often do you organize photo safaris?	**Mara ngapi mnafanya safari cha kupiga picha?**
What kinds of animals may be hunted?	**Tuna ruhusa ya kusaka aina gani ya wanyama mwitu?**

FOR GAME RESERVES, see page 183

RELAXING

antbear	mchimba chini
antelope	pofu
baboon	nyani
boar	nguruwe dume
buffalo	nyati
bushbaby *(monkey family)*	kombo
bushbuck	pongo
cheetah	duma
crocodile	mamba
dikdik *(antelope family)*	mgingi
duiker *(antelope family)*	funo
duck	bata
elephant	tembo [ndovu]
gazelle	swala
giraffe	twiga
hartebeest *(antelope family)*	kongoni
hippopotamus	kiboko
honey badger	nyerege
hyena	fisi
impala *(antelope family)*	swela
jackal	mbweha
kudu *(antelope family)*	tandala
greater kudu	tandala mkubwa
leopard	chui
lion/lioness	simba/simba jike
mongoose	nguchiro
monkey	nyani
colobus monkey	mbega
vervet monkey	tumbili
oryx *(antelope family)*	choroa
otter	fisi maji
porcupine	nungunungu
python	chatu
reedbuck *(antelope family)*	tohe
rhinoceros	kifaru
serval cat	mondo
snake	nyoka
squirrel (ground)/(bush)	kidiri/kindi
steinbok *(wild goat)*	tondoro
tortoise/turtle	kobe/kasa
warthog	ngiri
waterbuck *(antelope family)*	kuru
wild cat	paka wa mwitu
wild dog	mbwa mwitu
zebra	punda milia

Camping—Countryside

Camping can be a way of life in East Africa. The local people think of a tent as an air-conditioned hotel! So if your motto is "don't fence me in", why not join them?

You'll get a list of camping sites from the following organizations: Game Department, Nairobi, Tanzania National Tourist Board, Dar es Salaam, and Uganda Tourist Association, Kampala.

If you want to camp on private land, you need the owner's permission.

In Kenya and Tanzania, there are also some youth hostels.

Can we camp here?	**Tunaweza kupiga kambi hapa?**
Where can one camp for the night?	**Wapi tunaweza kupiga kambi kwa usiku?**
Is there a camping site near here?	**Papo mahali maalum pa kupiga kambi hapa?**
May we camp in your field?	**Tunaweza kupiga kambi shambani mwako?**
Can we park our caravan (trailer) here?	**Tunaweza kuacha karavani yetu hapa?**
Is this an official camping-site?	**Hapa mahali pa desturi pa kupiga kambi?**
May we light a fire?	**Tunaweza kuwasha moto?**
Is drinking water available?	**Yapo maji ya kunywa?**
Are there shopping facilities on the site?	**Yapo maduka mahali hapa?**
Are there ... ?	**Kuna ...?**
baths	**bafu la kuogea**
showers	**bomba la maji rasharasha**
toilets	**vyoo**

FOR CAMPING EQUIPMENT, see page 106

What's the charge ...?	Gharama yake ... nini?
per day	kwa kila siku
per person	kwa kila mtu
for a car	kwa gari
for a tent	kwa hema
for a caravan (trailer)	kwa karavani

Is there a youth hostel near here?	Ipo hoteli ya vijana hapa karibu?
Do you know anyone who can put us up for the night?	Unamjua mtu anayeweza kutupa mahali pa kulala usiku?

HAPANA KAMBI
NO CAMPING

HAPANA KARAVANI
NO CARAVANS (TRAILERS)

Landmarks

barn	ghala ya nafaka
bridge	daraja
brook	kijito
building	jumba
canal	mfereji
church	kanisa
cliff	jabali
copse	kichaka
cottage	kibanda
crossroads	njia panda
desert	jangwa
farm	shamba
ferry	feri
field	uwanja
footpath	njia ya miguu
forest	mwitu [pori]
hamlet	kitongoji
highway	barabara kuu
hill	kilima
house	nyumba
inn	nyumba ya wageni
jungle	mwitu

CAMPING – COUNTRYSIDE

lake	**ziwa**
marsh	**bwawa [ziwa lenye matope]**
moorland	**myika**
mountain	**mlima**
mountain range	**safu ya milima**
oasis	**chemchemi ya jangwa**
path	**njia**
peak	**kilele**
plantation	**bustani**
pond	**kiziwa**
pool	**kidimbwi**
railway	**njia ya gari la moshi [reli]**
river	**mto**
road	**barabara**
savannah	**nyika**
sea	**bahari**
spring	**chemchemi**
swamp	**ziwa la matope**
track	**njia ya gari la moshi**
tree	**mti**
valley	**bonde**
village	**kijiji [mtaa]**
vineyard	**shamba la mizabibu**
water	**maji**
waterfall	**maporomoko ya maji**
well	**kisima**
wood	**kuni [msitu]**

What's the name of that river?	**Nini jina la mto ule?**
How high is that mountain?	**Mlima ule una urefu gani?**

Hitch-hiking is not a very practical way of covering a planned itinerary in East Africa, since vehicles are still relatively rare in some areas. However, it is practised, and your patience will be rewarded by many a motorist more than happy to give you a lift.

Can you give me a lift to …?	**Unaweza kunichukua garini kwenda …?**

Making friends

Introductions

Here are a few phrases to get you started.

How do you do?	**Habari zako?**
How are you?	**Uhali gani?**
Very well, thank you.	**Sijambo sana.**
Fine, thanks. And you?	**Nzuri sana. Na wewe, hujambo?**
May I introduce Miss Philips?	**Nikutambulishe kwa Bi. Philips?**
I'd like you to meet a friend of mine.	**Napenda uonane na rafiki yangu.**
John, this is ...	**John, huyu ni ...**
My name is ...	**Jina langu ni ...**
Glad to know you.	**Nimefurahi kukujua.**

Follow-up

How long have you been here?	**Muda gani umekuwapo hapa?**
We've been here a week.	**Tumekuwa hapa muda wa wiki.**
Is this your first visit?	**Hii ni ziara yako ya kwanza?**
No, we came here last year.	**Hapana, tulikuja hapa mwaka jana.**
Are you on your own?	**Uko peke yako?**
I'm with ...	**Mimi nipo pamoja na ...**
my husband	**mume wangu**
my wife	**mke wangu**
my family	**jamaa yangu**
my parents	**wazee wangu**
some friends	**marafiki**

Where do you come from?	**Unatoka wapi?**
I'm from ...	**Natoka ...**
I'm a student.	**Mimi ni mwanafunzi**
What are you studying?	**Unasomea nini?**
We're here on holiday.	**Tupo hapa kwa mapumziko.**
I'm here on a business trip.	**Nipo hapa kwa shughuli za kazi.**
What kind of business are you in?	**Una shughuli za aina gani?**
I hope we'll see you again soon.	**Nataraji tutakuona mara nyingine karibuni.**
See you later/See you tomorrow.	**Tutaonana baadaye/Tutaonana kesho.**

The weather

They talk about the weather just as much in Africa as the Americans and the British are supposed to do. So ...

Is it usually as warm as this?	**Kuna joto hivi kwa kawaida?**
What awful weather.	**Hali ya hewa mbaya.**
It's very dusty, isn't it?	**Kuna mavumbi sana, ama sivyo?**
Do you think it'll ... tomorrow?	**Unafikiri ita ... kesho?**
rain	**nyesha mvua**
clear up	**safika hewa**
be sunny	**toka jua**

Invitations

My wife and I would like you to dine with us on ...	**Mimi na mke wangu tunapenda ule na sisi siku ya ...**
Can you come to dinner tomorrow night?	**Utaweza kuja kula na sisi kesho chakula cha jioni?**
We're giving a small party tomorrow night. I do hope you can come.	**Tunafanya karamu ndogo kesho usiku. Natumaini utaweza kuja.**
Can you come over for cocktails this evening?	**Unaweza kuja tunywe pamoja [cocktails] jioni ya leo?**
There's a party. Are you coming?	**Kuna karamu. Utakuja?**
That's very kind of you.	**Huo ndio wema wako.**
Great. I'd love to come.	**Vizuri. Nitapenda kuja.**
What time shall we come?	**Saa ngapi unataka tuje?**
May I bring a friend?	**Naweza kuja na rafiki?**
I'm afraid we've got to go now.	**Nasikitika lazima twende sasa.**
Next time you must come to visit us.	**Lazima utuzuru mara nyingine pia.**
Thanks for the evening. It was great fun.	**Asante kwa karamu hii. Ilipendeza sana.**

Dating

Would you like a cigarette?	**Unapenda sigara?**
Do you have a light, please?	**Unacho kibiriti, tafadhali?**
Can I get you a drink?	**Naweza kukuletea kinywaji?**
I'm lost. Can you show me the way to ... ?	**Nimepotea. Unaweza kunionesha njia ya kwenda ... ?**

Are you waiting for someone?	**Unamsubiri mtu fulani?**
Are you free this evening?	**Utapatikana jioni ya leo?**
Would you like to go out with me tonight?	**Unapenda kwenda nje na mimi usiku wa leo?**
Would you like to go dancing?	**Unapenda wenda kucheza dansi?**
I know a good discotheque.	**Napajua [discotheque] mahali pa dansi pazuri.**
Shall we go to the cinema (movies)?	**Twende senema?**
I'd love to, thank you.	**Napenda sana, asante.**
Where shall we meet?	**Tukutane wapi?**
I'll pick you up at your hotel.	**Nitakuchukua kutoka hoteli yako.**
I'll call for you at 8.	**Nitakupitia saa 2.**
May I take you home?	**Naweza kukuchukua nyumbani?**
Can I see you again tomorrow?	**Naweza kukuona tena kesho?**
Thank you, it's been a wonderful evening.	**Asante, ilikuwa jioni ya kustaajabisha.**
What's your telephone number?	**Nimi nambari yako ya simu?**
Do you live alone?	**Unaishi peke yako?**
What time is your last bus?	**Saa ngapi basi yako ya mwisho?**

FOR TIME OF DAY, see page 177

Shopping guide

This shopping guide is designed to help you find what you want—with ease, accuracy and speed. It features:

1. a list of all major shops, stores and services;
2. some general expressions required when shopping—to allow you to be specific and selective;
3. full details of the shops and services most likely to concern you. Here you'll find advice and alphabetical lists of items under the headings below.

		Page
Bookshop	books, magazines, newspapers, stationery	104
Camping	camping equipment and cooking utensils	106
Chemist's (drugstore)	medicine, first-aid, cosmetics, toilet articles	108
Clothing	clothes, shoes, accessories	112
Electrical appliances	radios, tape recorders, shavers, records	119
Hairdresser's	barber's, ladies' hairdresser's, beauty salon	121
Jeweller's	jewellery, watches, watch repairs	123
Laundry—Dry cleaning	usual facilities	126
Photography	cameras, accessories, films, developing	127
Provisions	this is confined to basic items required for picnics	129
Souvenirs	souvenirs, gifts, fancy goods	131
Tobacconist's	smoker's supplies	133

SHOPPING GUIDE

Advice

If you have a pretty clear idea what you want before you set out, do a little homework first. Look under the appropriate heading, pick out the article and find a suitable description for it (colour, material, etc.). If you just happen to wander into a shop, turn to the appropriate heading and tackle the conversation step by step, as shown.

In East Africa, the smaller shops usually open at 8.30 a.m. and close at 8 p.m. Some close for lunch at noon and open again at 3 p.m. Department stores normally open at 9 a.m. and stay open during lunch hours. All shops are open on Saturdays until 2 p.m. Very few shops are open on Sundays or public holidays.

In addition to shops, outdoor markets flourish in every East African town. In the larger cities there are food markets, handicraft markets, etc. Haggling is acceptable in the markets and small shops, but not in the larger stores, which have fixed prices.

Shops, stores and services

Where's the nearest ...?	Liko wapi .... lililo karibu?
art gallery	duka la michoro ya picha
baker's	duka la mikate
bank	benki
barber's	kinyozi
beauty salon	duka la urembo wa kike
bookshop	duka la vitabu
butcher's	duka la nyama
camera store	duka la kamera
candy store	duka la halua na kashata
chemist's	duka la dawa
confectioner's	duka la halua na kashata
dairy	duka la vitu yva maziwa
dentist	daktari wa meno
department store	duka la aina ya kila kitu

doctor	**daktari**
dressmaker	**mshonaji nguo**
drugstore	**duka la dawa**
dry cleaner	**dobi wa nguo za sufi**
dry goods store	**duka la vyombo**
fishmonger's	**soko ya samaki**
florist	**muuzaji maua**
greengrocer	**duka la mboga na matunda**
grocery	**duka la vyakula**
hairdresser (men)	**kinyozi wa wanaume**
hairdresser (ladies)	**kinyozi wa wanawake**
hardware store	**duka la vyombo vya chuma**
hat shop	**duka la chapeo [kofia]**
health food shop	**duka la vyakula vya afya [siha]**
hospital	**hospitali**
ironmonger	**duka la vyombo vya chuma**
jeweller	**sonara wa madini**
laundry	**mahali pa kufulia nguo**
leather goods store	**duka la vitu vya ngozi**
liquor store	**duka la vileo**
market	**soko**
newsagent	**duka la magazeti**
news-stand	**muuzaji magazeti**
off-licence	**duka la vileo (masandukuni)**
optician	**daktari wa macho**
pastry shop	**duka la maandazi**
pawnbroker	**duka la rehani**
pharmacy	**duka la dawa**
photo shop	**duka la kupiga picha**
police station	**stesheni ya polisi**
post office	**ofisi ya posta**
shoe shop	**duka la viatu**
souvenir shop	**duka la vitu vya ukumbusho**
sporting goods shop	**duka la vyombo vya michezo ya spoti**
stationer	**muuzaji kalamu na karatasi**
supermarket	**duka la soko kuu**
tailor's	**mshonaji**
telegraph office	**ofisi ya kupeleka simu**
tobacconist	**duka la tumbaku**
toy shop	**duka la vitu vya kitoto**
travel agent	**wakili wa safari**
watchmaker's	**duka la mtengenezaji wa saa**

General expressions

Here are some expressions which will be useful to you when you're out shopping.

Where?

Where's a good ... shop?	**Lipo wapi duka zuri la ...?**
Where can I find a ...?	**Wapi nitaona ...?**
Can you recommend an inexpensive ...?	**Unaweza kunisifia ... iliyo rahisi?**
Where's the main shopping area?	**Wapi mahali hasa pa maduka?**
How far is it from here?	**Umbali gani kutoka hapa?**

Service

Can you help me?	**Unaweza kunisaidia?**
I'm just looking around.	**Naangalia tu.**
I want ...	**Nataka ...**
Can you show me some ...?	**Unaweza kunionyesha ...?**
Do you have any ...?	**Unayo ...?**

That one

Can you show me ...?	**Unaweza kunionesha ...?**
that/those	**ile/zile**
the one in the window	**ile iliyopo dirishani**
the one in the display case	**ile ndani ya sanduku la maonyesho**
It's over there.	**Ipo pale.**

Defining the article

I'd like a ...	Napenda ...
I want a ... one.	Nataka iliyo ...
big	kubwa
cheap	rahisi
dark	nyeusi
good	bora
heavy	nzito
large	kubwa
light (weight)	nyepesi
light (colour)	yenye kung'aa
oval	mviringo kama yai
rectangular	ya pembe za mraba
round	duara
small	ndogo
square	mraba
sturdy	nene
I don't want anything too expensive.	Sitaki kitu chochote kilicho ghali.

Preference

I prefer something of better quality.	Nitapenda kitu cha aina bora zaidi.
Can you show me some more?	Unaweza kunionyesha nyingine zaidi?
Haven't you anything ...?	Huna kitu chochote ...?
cheaper/better	rahisi zaidi/bora
larger/smaller	kubwa zaidi/ndogo zaidi

How much?

How much is this?	Bei [Kiasi] gani hii?
I don't understand.	Sielewi.
Please write it down.	Tafadhali andika bei.
I don't want to spend more than ...	Sitaki kutumia zaidi ya ...

FOR COLOURS, see page 113

SHOPPING GUIDE

Decision

That's just what I want.	**Hiyo ndiyo hasa ninayoitaka.**
It's not quite what I want.	**Si hiyo ninayoitaka hasa.**
No, I don't like it.	**Hapana, siipendi.**
I'll take it.	**Nitaichukua.**

Ordering

Can you order it for me?	**Unaweza kuagiza kwa ajili yangu?**
How long will it take?	**Muda gani itachukua?**
I'd like it as soon as possible.	**Ningeitaka kwa haraka iwezekanavyo.**

Delivery

I'll take it with me.	**Nitaichukua pamoja nami.**
Deliver it to the ...Hotel.	**Niletee huko ...Hotel.**
Will I have any difficulty with the customs?	**Nitapata taabu yeyote na idara ya ushuru?**

Paying

How much is it?	**Bei [Kiasi] gani?**
Can I pay by traveller's cheque?	**Naweza kulipa kwa cheki ya wasafiri?**
Do you accept dollars/ pounds?	**Unapokea malipo kwa dola/ pauni ya Kiingereza?**
Do you accept credit cards?	**Unapokea malipo kwa kadi ya benki?**
Do you have a carrier (shopping) bag/box?	**Unayo bahasha ya kuchukulia/ boksi?**

FOR NUMBERS, see page 175

Anything else?

No, thanks, that's all.	**Asante, hiyo inatosha.**
Yes, I want ...	**Ndiyo, nataka ...**
Show me ...	**Nionyeshe ...**
Thank you. Good-bye.	**Asante. Kwa heri.**

Dissatisfied

Can you please exchange this?	**Tafadhali unaweza kuibadilisha hii?**
I want to return this.	**Nataka kuirejesha hii.**
I'd like a refund. Here's the receipt.	**Napenda unirejeshee pesa. Hii ni risiti.**

Naweza kukusaidia?	Can I help you?
Nini utapenda?	What would you like?
...gani utapenda?	What... would you like?
rangi/namna aina/kadiri	colour/shape quality/quantity
Samahani, hatuna hata.	I'm sorry, we haven't any.
Tumeishiwa na yote.	We're out of stock.
Tuagize kwa ajili yako?	Shall we order it for you?
Utaichukua au tutakuleta?	Will you take it with you or shall we send it?
Haja yeyote nyengine?	Anything else?
Hiyo hi shilingi ...	That's... shillings, please.
Mpokeaji pesa yupo pale.	The cashier's over there.

SHOPPING GUIDE

Bookshop—Stationer's—News-stand

English-language newspapers and magazines are on sale in all leading East African cities. International editions of news magazines are available in the better hotels. Local English-language dailies are published in all major cities.

Bookshops and stationers are one and the same thing in East Africa. News-stands and newsboys can be found everywhere.

Where's the nearest ...?	Liko wapi ... lililo karibu?
bookshop/stationer's	duka la vitabu
news-stand	muuzaji magazeti
Can you recommend a good bookshop?	Unaweza kunisifia duka zuri la vitabu?
Where can I buy an English newspaper?	Wapi naweza kununua gazeti la Kiingereza?
I want to buy a/an/some ...	Nataka kununua ...
address book	buku la kuandika anuani
ball-point pen	kalamu ya tufe
book	kitabu
box of paints	boksi la kalamu za rangi
carbon paper	karatasi ya kukopia
cellophane tape	utepe wa gundi
crayons	chaki za rangi
dictionary	kamusi
Swahili-English	ya Kiswahili kwa Kiingereza
English-Swahili	ya Kiingereza kwa Kiswahili
drawing paper	karatasi ya kuchorea picha
drawing pins	pini za kubania
envelopes	bahasha za barua
eraser	raba ya kufutia
exercise book	daftari
file	faili
fountain pen	kalamu ya wino
glue	gundi
grammar book	kitabu cha sarufi
guide book	kitabu cha matembezi ya mji

ink	wino
black/red/blue	mweusi/mwekundu/buluu
labels	label
magazine	gazeti la picha na habari
map	ramani
map of the town	ramani ya mji
road map of ...	ramani ya njia ya ...
newspaper	gazeti la
American/English	Kimarekani/Kiingereza
notebook	daftari kuandikia ndogo ya
note paper	karatasi ya kuandikia
paperback	kitabu rahisi
paper napkins	anjifu za karatasi
paste	gundi
pen	kalamu
pencil	penseli
pencil sharpener	kijembe cha penseli
playing cards	karata
postcards	picha za kutuma posta
refill (for a pen)	wino tayari
rubber	raba ya kufutia
ruler	msitari
sketching pad	ubao wa kuchorea
string	uzi
thumbtacks	pini za kubania
tissue paper	anjifu za karatasi
tracing paper	karatasi za kunakilia
typewriter ribbon	utepe wa taipu
typing paper	karatasi za taipu
wrapping paper	karatasi za kufungia vitu
writing pad	karatasi za kuandikia

Where's the guide-book section?	Iko wapi idara ya vitabu vya utalii?
Is there an English translation of ...?	Unacho kitabu cha ... kilichofasiriwa kwa Kiingereza?
Where do you keep the English books?	Wapi unaweka vitabu vya Kiingereza?

Camping

Here we're concerned with the equipment you may need.

I'd like a/an/some …	Nataka …
axe	shoka
bottle-opener	kifunguo cha chupa
bucket	ndoo
butane gas	butugas
camp bed	kitanda cha kambi
camping equipment	vyombo vya kambi
can opener	kifunguo cha kopo
candles	mishumaa
chair	kiti
folding chair	kiti cha kukunja
compass	dira
corkscrew	ufunguo wa kizibo cha chupa
crockery	sahani na vikombe
cutlery	visu na vijiko
deck-chair	kiti cha kulala
first-aid kit	vyombo vya kutibu jeraha
fishing tackle	zana za kuvulia samaki
flashlight	tochi
frying-pan	sufuria ya kukaangia
groundsheet	foronya ya kukalia chini
hammer	nyundo
hammock	wavu wa kulalia
haversack	mkoba
ice-bag	mfuko wa barafu
kerosene	mafuta ya taa
kettle	birika ya chai
knapsack	mkoba wa safari
lamp	taa
lantern	taa ya mkono
matches	kiberiti
mattress	godoro
methylated spirits	dawa ya mbao
mosquito net	chandarua cha mbu
pail	ndoo
paraffin	mafuta ya taa
penknife	kisu cha mfuko
picnic case	kasha la mandari
pressure cooker	sufuria ya stimu ya wali
primus stove	jiko la stovu

rope	kamba
rucksack	mfuko wa begani
saucepan	sufuria ndogo
scissors	mkasi
screwdriver	bisibisi
sheathknife	kisu chenye ala
sleeping bag	mfuko wa kulalia
stewpan	sufuria ya mchuzi
stove	jiko, stovu
table	meza
folding table	meza ya kukunja
tent	hema
tent-peg	vigingi vya hema
tent-pole	nguzo ya hema
thermos flask (bottle)	chupa ya kuwekea chai
tin-opener	kifungua cha kopo
tongs	koleo
tool kit	zana kamili za ufundi
torch	tochi
water carrier	kigari cha kubebea maji
wood alcohol	dawa ya mbao

Crockery

beakers (tumblers)	vikombe vya kunywea
cups	vikombe
food box	boksi la vyakula
mugs	makopo
plates	sahani
saucers	visahani vya vikombe

Cutlery

forks	uma
knives	visu
dessert knife	kisu cha matunda
spoons	vijiko
teaspoons	vijiko vya chai
(made of) plastic	(vya) plastiki
(made of) stainless steel	(vya) chuma safi

Chemist's (drugstore)

Pharmaceutical supplies pose no problem for visitors. All major cities have excellent chemists'. Some chemists' stock strictly medical goods but the larger ones have a wider range of articles.

You can get along in English for the names of most medicinal products.

This section has been divided into two parts:

1. Pharmaceutical: medicine, first-aid, etc.
2. Toiletry: toilet articles, cosmetics, etc.

General

Where's the nearest (all-night) chemist?	**Wapi duka la dawa (linalo fungukiwa usiku) hapa karibu?**
Can you recommend a good chemist?	**Unaweza kunisifia duka zuri la dawa?**
What time does the chemist open/close?	**Saa ngapi hufunguliwa/ hufungwa duka la dawa?**

Part 1 – Pharmaceutical

I want something for ...	**Nataka dawa ya ...**
a cold/cough	**kamasi/kikohozi**
hay fever	**homa ya makamasi**
a hangover	**maumivu ya kichwa**
sunburn	**kubabuka ngozi**
travel sickness	**kichefuchefu**
an upset stomach	**kuumwa tumbo**
Can you make up this prescription for me?	**Unaweza kunipatia dawa kwa amri hii ya daktari?**
Shall I wait?	**Je, nisubiri?**
When shall I come back?	**Wakati gani nirejee?**

FOR DOCTOR, see page 162

SHOPPING GUIDE

Can I get it without a prescription?	Naweza kuipata pasipo amri ya daktari?
Can I have a/an/some ...?	Naweza kupata ...?

ammonia	ammonia
antiseptic cream	dawa va kutoozesha jeraha
aspirin	spirini
bandage	kitambaa cha bendeji
crepe bandage	bendeji ilio pana
gauze bandage	bendeji ya shashi
Band-Aids	plasta ya jeraha
calcium tablets	vidonge vya dawa ya chokaa
castor oil	mafuta ya mbarika
chlorine tablets	vidonge vya klorin
contraceptives	dawa ya kuzuia mimba
corn plasters	plasta ya corn
cotton wool	pamba
cough drops	dawa ya kukohoa
diabetic lozenges	diabetic lozenges
disinfectant (bottle/tube)	(chupa/mrija) wa dawa ya kuua wadudu
ear drops	dawa ya masikio
Elastoplast	plasta ya jeraha
first-aid kit	vyombo vya kutibu jeraha
flea powder	podari ya kiroboto
gargle	dawa ya kusukutua
insect lotion	loshani ya vidudu
iodine	aidini
iron pills	vidonge vya nguvu
laxative	haluli
lint	lint [ya kutibu jeraha]
mouthwash	dawa ya mdomo
quinine tablets	vidonge vya kunini
sanitary napkins	bahasha za choo
sedative	dawa ya kutuliza
sleeping pills	dawa ya kulala
stomach pills	vidonge vya kutibu tumbo
surgical dressing	mafuta ya kutibu jeraha
thermometer	kipimo cha kupimia joto
throat lozenges	throat lozenges
tonic	tonic
tranquillizers	dawa ya kuondosha fahamu
vitamin pills	vidonge vya vitamin
weight-reducing tablets	vidonge vya kupunguza uzito

Part 2—Toiletry

I'd like a/an/some …	Nataka …
acne cream	dawa ya chunusi
after-shave lotion	mafuta ya kunyolea ndevu
bath cubes	vidonge vya kuogea
bath essence	marashi ya kuogea
bath salts	chumvi ya kuogea
cream	cream
cleansing cream	cleansing cream
cold cream	cream ya kupaka usoni
cuticle cream	cuticle cream
enzyme cream	enzyme cream
foundation cream	foundation cream
hormone cream	hormone cream
moisturizing cream	moisturizing cream
night cream	cream ya usiku
cuticle remover	dawa ya kubadilisha ngozi
deodorant	mafuta ya kwapa
eau de Cologne	de Cologne
emery board	ubao wa msasa
eye liner	wanja wa macho
eye shadow	rangi va macho
face pack	kiboksi cha vitu vya kusafisha uso
face powder	podari ya uso
foot cream/deodorant	cream/mafuta ya mguu
hand cream/lotion	cream/mafuta ya mkono
lipsalve	malhamu ya mdomo
lipstick	rangi ya mdomo
make-up remover pads	karatasi za kufutia urembo
mascara	maskara
nail brush	brashi ya kucha
nail clippers	kidude cha kukatia kucha
nail file	tupa ya kucha
nail polish	rangi ya kucha
nail polish remover	dawa ya kufutia rangi ya kucha
nail scissors	mkasi wa kucha
nail strengthener	dawa ya kukazisha kucha
perfume	manukato
powder	podari
powder puff	kibonge cha kupakia podari
pumice stone	jiwe jepesi
rouge	podari nyekundu ya usoni
safety pins	pini za kuvaa

shampoo	shampoo [dawa ya nywele]
cream/liquid	ya cream/ya maji
shaving brush	brashi ya kunyolea
shaving cream	sabuni ya kunyolea
shaving soap	sabuni ya kunyolea
soap	sabuni
sponge	spanji
sun-tan cream/oil	cream/mafuta ya kujipasha jua
talcum powder	podari ya mwili
tissues	anjifu za karatasi
toilet paper	karatasi ya kujifutia chooni
toilet water	maji ya kutumia chooni
toothbrush	mswaki wa meno
bristle/nylon	ya manyoya/ya nailoni
toothpaste	dawa ya kusafishia meno
toothpowder	podari ya meno
tweezers	kikoleo

For your hair

bobby pins	pini za nywele
brush	brashi ya nywele
curlers	pini za kufanya nywele mawimbi
dye/tint	rangi ya nywele
grips	vibano vya nywele
lacquer	rangi nyeusi
oil	mafuta ya nywele
pins	pini
rollers	pini za kuvurunga nywele
setting lotion	mafuta ya kusawazisha nywele

For the baby

beaker (tumbler)	kikombe cha kunywea cha mtoto
bib	kitambaa cha mtoto
cream	krimu ya mtoto
diapers	uwinda wa mtoto
dummy	kipira cha mtoto
food	chakula cha mtoto
nappies	uwinda wa mtoto
nappy pins	pini za uwinda
oil	mafuta ya mtoto
pacifier	kipira cha mtoto
plastic pants	suruali ya plastik ya mtoto
powder	podari ya mtoto

Clothing

If you have something specific in mind to buy, prepare yourself in advance. Look at the list of clothing on page 117. Get some idea of the colour, material and size you want. They're all listed on the next few pages.

For traditional local garments and shoes, see page 132.

General

I'd like ...	**Nataka ...**
I want ... for a 10-year-old boy.	**Nataka ... ya mtoto wa miaka 10.**
I want something like this.	**Nataka kitu kama hiki.**
I like the one in the window.	**Napenda ile iliopo dirishani.**
How much is that per yard?	**Bei [Kiasi] gani ile kwa kila yadi?**

1 centimetre	= 0.39 in.	1 inch	= 2.54 cm.
1 metre	= 39.37 in.	1 foot	= 30.5 cm.
10 metres	= 32.81 ft.	1 yard	= 0.91 m

Colour

I want something in ...	**Nataka yenye rangi ...**
I want a darker shade.	**Nataka ya weusi zaidi.**
I want something to match this.	**Nataka kitu kinachofanana na hiki.**
I don't like the colour.	**Sikuipenda rangi yake.**

beige	**rangi ya chicha**
black	**rangi nyeusi**
blue	**rangi ya buluu**
brown	**rangi ya hudhurungi [kahawia]**
cream	**rangi ya maziwa**
crimson	**rangi nyekundu ya damu**
emerald	**rangi ya zumaradi**
fawn	**rangi ya paa**
gold	**rangi ya dhahabu**
green	**rangi kijani**
grey	**rangi ya jivu**
mauve	**rangi ya urujuani**
orange	**rangi ya machungwa**
pink	**rangi ya sharubati**
purple	**rangi ya zambarau**
red	**rangi nyekundu**
scarlet	**rangi nyekundu iliyozagaa**
silver	**rangi ya fedha**
tan	**rangi ya kuungua**
turquoise	**rangi ya feruzi**
white	**rangi nyeupe**
yellow	**rangi manjano**

misumeno

wavu

**vidoto
[kanga]**

**mistari
ya mapana**

Material

Do you have anything in …?	**Una kitu chochote katika …?**
I want a cotton blouse.	**Nataka blauzi ya pamba.**
Is that …?	**Hiyo ime …?**
hand-made	**-fanywa kwa mkono**
imported	**-agizwa kutoka ng'ambo**
made here	**-fanywa hapa**
I want something thinner.	**Nataka ilio nyembamba zaidi.**
Do you have any better quality?	**Unayo ya aina bora?**

What's it made of?	**Imefanywa kwa kitu gani?**

It may be made of …

baboon skin	**manyoya ya nyani**
cambric	**katani nyepesi**
camel hide	**manyoya ya ngamia**
chiffon	**shifoni**
colobus monkey skin	**manyoya ya mbega**
corduroy	**kodoroi**
cotton	**pamba [katani]**
crepe	**shashi**
felt	**manyoya na sherizi**
flannel	**manyoya ya kondoo**
gabardine	**gabadini**
lace	**kimia**
leather	**ngozi**
leopard skin	**manyoya ya chui**
linen	**kitani**
needlecord	**uzi wa sindano**
nylon	**nailoni**
piqué	**mchanganyo**
poplin	**poplini**
rayon	**rayon [nailoni ya mpira]**
rubber	**mpira**
satin	**satin**
serge	**sufi ya kondoo**
silk	**hariri**
tussore silk (coarse silk)	**lasi**
sisal	**ukonge**
suede	**ngozi nyepesi**
taffeta	**tafeta**
tweed	**manyoya ya kondoo**
velvet	**mahameli**
velveteen	**mfano wa mahameli**
velvet monkey skin	**manyoya ya tumbili**
wool	**sufu**
worsted	**uzi wa sufu**

Size

My size is 38.	**Kadiri yangu ni 38.**
Our sizes are different at home. Could you measure me?	**Nambari za kadiri ni tafauti kule nyumbani. Unaweza kunipima?**

This is your size

All East African countries use British sizes.

In Europe as well as in East Africa and America, sizes vary somewhat from country to country, so the charts below must be taken as an approximate guide.

Ladies

Dresses/suits						
American	10	12	14	16	18	20
British/ East African	32	34	36	38	40	42
Continental	38	40	42	44	46	48

	Stockings						Shoes				
American							6	$6^1/_2$ 7	8		$8^1/_2$
British/ East African	8	$8^1/_2$ 9	$9^1/_2$ 10	$10^1/_2$			$4^1/_2$	5	$5^1/_2$ $6^1/_2$	7	
Continental	0	1	2	3	4	5	36	37	38	$38^1/_2$	39

Gentlemen

Suits/overcoats						
American British/ East African	36	38	40	42	44	46
Continental	46	48	50	52	54	56

Shirts							
American British/ East African	14	$14^1/_2$ 15	$15^1/_2$ 16	$16^1/_2$ 17			$17^1/_2$
Continental	36	37	38	39	41	42	43	44

Shoes								
American British/ East African	5	6	7	8	$8^1/_2$	9	$9^1/_2$	10	11
Continental	38	39	41	42	43	43	44	44	45

FOR NUMBERS, see page 175

SHOPPING GUIDE

A good fit?

Can I try it on?	Naweza kuijaribu mwilini?
Where's the fitting room?	Wapi chumba cha kuvalia?
Is there a mirror?	Kipo kioo?
Does it fit?	Eti inanifaa?
It fits very well.	Inanifaa vizuri sana.
It doesn't fit.	Haifai.
It's too ...	Ni ... sana.
short/long	fupi/ndefu
tight/loose	inabana/inapwaya
How long will it take to alter?	Muda gani itachukua kuibadilisha?

Shoes

I'd like a pair of ...	Nataka ...
shoes/sandals	viatu/champali
boots/slippers	buti/sapatu
These are too ...	Hivi vi ... sana.
narrow/wide	-nakaza/-pana
large/small	-kubwa/-dogo
They pinch my toes.	Vinabana vidole vyangu.
Do you have a larger size?	Unavyo vya kadiri kubwa?
I want a smaller size.	Nataka vya kadiri ndogo.
Do you have the same in ...?	Unavyo namna hiyo vya rangi ...?
black/brown/white	nyeusi/hudhurungi/nyeupe

Shoes worn out? Here's the key to getting them fixed again:

Can you repair these shoes?	Unaweza kutengeneza viatu hivi?
I want new soles and heels.	Nataka soli mpya na visigino.
When will they be ready?	Wakati gani vitakuwa tayari?

Clothes and accessories

I would like a/an/some ...   Nataka ...

anorak	koti fupi la mvua
bathing cap	kofia ya kuogea
bathing suit	nguo za kuogea
bathrobe	taulo ya kuvaa
blazer	koti la kazi
blouse	blauzi
braces	ukanda
briefs	andawia ya kike
cap	kofia
handmade cap	kofia ya mkono
embroidered cap	kofia iliofumwa
cape	vazi la kuvaa mabegani
cardigan	sweta
coat	koti
dinner jacket	koti rasmi la chejio
dress	kanzu ya kike
dressing gown	gauni
evening dress (woman's)	kanzu ya usiku y kike
fez	tarabushi
frock	kanzu ya kike
fur coat	koti la manyoya
garters	ukanda wa soksi
girdle	mshipi
gloves	glavu
gym shoes	viatu vya spoti
handkerchief	anjifu
hat	chepeo
housecoat	koti la kuvaa nyumbani
jacket	jeketi
jersey	jaasi
jumper (Br.)	sweta zito
lingerie	kanzu ya ndani ya kike
mackintosh	koti la mvua
nightdress	vazi la usiku
overalls	dangrizi
overcoat	koti la baridi
panties	suruali fupi
pants	suruali
pants suit	suti ya suruali
panty girdle	ukanda wa suruali
panty hose	soksi ndefu za suruali
petticoat	kizibao

pullover	**sweta nzito**
pyjamas	**pajama**
raincoat	**koti la mvua**
robe	**gauni [joho]**
rubber boots	**viatu vya mpira**
sandals	**ndara**
leather sandals	**makubazi**
scarf	**skafu**
shirt	**shati**
shoes	**viatu**
shorts	**suruali fupi**
skirt	**skati**
slacks	**suruali ya kike**
slip	**smizi**
slippers	**sapatu**
socks	**soksi**
sports jacket	**koti la spoti**
stockings	**soksi ndefu**
suit (man's)	**suti ya kiume**
suit (woman's)	**suiti ya kike**
suspender belt	**ukanda wa kuvuta**
suspenders	**ukanda**
sweatshirt	**shati la sweta**
swimsuit	**nguo za kuogea**
T-shirt	**shati la fulana**
tennis shoes	**viatu vya kuchezea tennis**
tights	**skati ya kubana**
track suit	**suti ya kupandia farasi**
trousers	**suruali**
underpants (men's)	**andawia ya kike**
undershirt	**shati la ndani [fulana]**
vest (Am.)	**fulana ya mkono mfupi**
vest (Br.)	**fulana ya mkono**
waistcoat	**kikoti cha ndani**

belt	**mkanda [mshipi]**
buckle	**kifungo**
cuffs	**vifungo vya mkono wa shati**
elastic	**mpira wa kuvuta**
hem	**mpindo**
lapel	**kitambaa cha mawimbi**
lining	**kitambaa cha ndani ya kanzu**
pocket	**mfuko**
ribbon	**ribini**
sleeve	**mkono**

FOR LOCAL CLOTHES, see page 132

Electrical appliances and accessories—Records

Not all parts of East Africa are served by electric power. Most major towns, however, are supplied with 220-volt AC current. Smaller towns and some villages have local power generators which vary in voltage.

Tourist hotels generally provide an adaptor for 220 and 110 volts. The plug in use throughout East Africa is of the three-pin type. Consult the hotel management first before plugging in your adaptor or appliance. It's also advisable to take along a screw-in adaptor to fit into light-bulb sockets.

What's the voltage?	**Voltage nambari ngapi hapa?**
Is it AC or DC?	**Ni AC au DC?**
I want a plug for this ...	**Nataka plagi ya hii ...**
Do you have a battery for this ...?	**Unayo betri ya hii ...**
This is broken. Can you repair it?	**Hii imevunjika. Unaweza kuitengeneza?**
When will it be ready?	**Lini itakuwa tayari?**
I'd like a/an/some ...	**Nataka ...**
adaptor	**edepta**
amplifier	**bomba la sauti**
battery	**beteri**
blender	**mtambo wa kuchanganya**
fan	**panka boi**
food mixer	**mtambo wa kuvuruga [kukoroga]chakula**
hair dryer	**mtambo wa kukausha nywele**
iron	**pasi**
travelling-iron	**pasi ya safari**
kettle	**birika la moto**
percolator	**birika la kupikia kahawa**
plug	**plagi**
radio	**radio**
car radio	**radio ya gari**
portable radio	**radio ya mkono**

record player	**santuri**
portable record player	**santuri ndogo**
tape recorder	**tape recorder**
cassette tape recorder	**tape recorder ya cassette**
portable tape recorder	**tape recorder ndogo ya safari**
television	**televisheni**
portable television	**televisheni ya mkono**
toaster	**mtambo wa kufaniya tosti**
transformer	**transfoma**

Record shop

Western classical music as well as pop hits can be purchased in all major towns. Records aren't produced locally in stereo yet, and most are 45 r.p.m. cuttings. The Swahili expression for record is *sahani ya santuri* but you can also get away with *rekodi*.

Do you have any records by ...?	**Unazo rekodi za nyimbo za ...?**
Do you have...'s latest album?	**Unayo jamii ya nyimbo mpya za ...?**
Can I listen to this record?	**Naweza kuisikia rekodi hii?**
I'd like a cassette.	**Nataka cassette ya tepu.**
I want a new needle.	**Nataka sindano mpya.**

L.P.	**sahani kubwa**
33/45 rpm	**sahani ya 33/45**
mono/stereo	**mono/stirio**

chamber music	**muziki wa chamber**
classical music	**muziki wa classic**
folk music	**muziki wa kitamaduni**
instrumental music	**muziki usio na maneno**
jazz	**jaz**
light music	**muziki wa kuburudisha**
orchestral music	**muziki wa tarabu**
pop music	**muziki wa kisasa**

Hairdressing—Barber's

I don't speak much Swahili.	**Sisemi Kiswahili vizuri.**
I'm in a hurry.	**Nina haraka.**
I want a haircut, please.	**Tafadhali nikate nywele.**
I'd like a shave.	**Nataka kunyoa ndevu.**
Don't cut it too short.	**Usikate fupi sana.**
Scissors only, please.	**Kata kwa mkasi tu.**
A razor cut, please.	**Nyoa kwa wembe, tafadhali.**
Don't use the clippers.	**Usitumie mashini ya kinyozi.**
Just a trim, please.	**Zitengeneze kidogo tu.**
That's enough off.	**Umekata za kutosha.**
A little more off the ...	**Kata zaidi kidogo hapa ...**
back	**nyuma**
neck	**shingoni**
sides	**pembeni**
top	**juu**
I don't want any cream.	**Sitaki krimu yoyote.**
Please don't use any oil.	**Tafadhali usitumie mafuta.**
Would you please trim my ...?	**Unaweza kutengeneza ...zangu**
beard	**ndevu**
moustache	**sharubu**
sideboards (sideburns)	**nywele za shavuni**
Thank you. That's fine.	**Asante. Hii inapendeza.**
How much do I owe you?	**Nilipe kiasi gani?**
This is for you.	**Hii ni bakshishi yako.**

Ladies' hairdressing

Is there a beauty salon in the hotel?	**Lipo duka la mapambo hapa hotelini?**
Can I make an appointment for some-time on Thursday?	**Naweza kuja wakati wowote siku ya alhamisi.**
I'd like it cut and shaped	**Nataka uzikate na uzilengeshe.**

with a fringe (bangs)	**fanya kishungi**
page-boy style	**fupi na mstari wa kati**
a razor cut	**kata kwa wembe**
a re-style	**staili mpya**
with ringlets	**zungurusha chini**
with waves	**zenye mawimbi**
in a bun	**fanya kirungu nyuma**
braided	**suka**

I want a ...	**Nataka ...**
bleach	**rangi ya hudhurungi**
colour rinse	**uzipake rangi**
dye	**ubadilishe rangi**
permanent	**ziwe daima**
shampoo and set	**kuosha kwa shampuu kama hivyo**
tint	**hudhurungi ya kung'aa**
touch up	**zigusishe na rangi**
the same colour	**rangi kama ya sasa**
a darker colour	**rangi iliokoza zaidi**
a lighter colour	**rangi isiyong'aa**
auburn/blond	**kama hudhurungi/rangi ya shaba**
brunette	**hudhurungi iliokoza na weusi**
Do you have a colour chart?	**Unacho kitabu cha aina ya rangi?**
I don't want any hairspray.	**Sitaki dawa ya kupulizia nywele.**
I want a ...	**Nataka urembo wa ...**
manicure/pedicure/face-pack	**mikono/miguu/uso**

Jeweller's—Watchmaker's

East African jewellers prefer to concentrate on their artistic handwork rather than dealing with watches. Every jeweller is proud of the variety of designs he can offer his customers. One rare characteristic peculiar to East African jewellers is that they're personally at their customers'disposal. Their shops, not numerous, are usually small.

Can you repair this watch?	**Unaweza kuitengeneza saa hii?**
The ... is broken.	**... imevunjika.**
glass/spring strap/winder	**kioo/kamani ukanda/ufunguo**
I want this watch cleaned.	**Nataka saa hii isafishwe.**
When will it be ready?	**Siku gani itakuwa tayari?**
Could I please see that?	**Naweza kuiona ile?**
I'm just looking around.	**Natazama duka tu.**
I want a small present for ...	**Nataka zawadi ndogo kwa ...**
I don't want anything too expensive.	**Sitaki kitu chochote kilicho ghali mno.**
I want something ...	**Nataka kitu kilicho ...**
better/cheaper/simpler	**bora/rahisi/kidogo**
Is this real silver?	**Je hii fedha safi?**
Do you have anything in gold?	**Unacho kitu cha dhahabu?**

If it's made of gold, ask:

How many carats is this?	**Kereti ngapi hii?**

When you go to a jeweller's, you've probably got some idea of what you want beforehand. Find out what the article is made of and then look up the name of the article in the following lists.

What's it made of?

amber	**emba**
amethyst	**amethyst**
chromium	**krom**
copper	**shaba nyekundu**
coral	**marijani**
crystal	**jiwe la kung'aa**
cut glass	**kioo kilichokatwa**
diamond	**almasi**
ebony	**mpingo**
emerald	**zumaradi**
enamel	**mpako wa kung'aa**
glass	**kioo kilichokatwa**
gold	**dhahabu**
gold leaf	**jani la dhahabu**
ivory	**pembe**
jade	**jiwe la thamani la kijani**
onyx	**kito cha rangi**
pearl	**lulu**
pewter	**madini**
platinum	**madini nyeupe**
ruby	**kito chekundu**
sapphire	**johari ya samawati**
silver	**fedha**
silver plate	**fedha asili**
stainless steel	**chuma cha pua**
topaz	**yakuti manjano**
turquoise	**madini feruzi**

What is it?

bangle	**bangili**
beads	**ushanga**
bracelet	**kidani**
charm bracelet	**kidani**
brooch	**kifungo**
chain	**mkufu**
charm	**talasimu [hirizi]**
cigarette case	**mfuko wa sigareti**
cigarette lighter	**kiberiti cha sigareti cha mafuta**
clip	**klipu [kibano]**

clock	saa
alarm clock	saa ya kengele
travelling-clock	saa ya kusafiria
collar stud	kifungo cha kola
cross	msalaba
cuff-links	vifungo vya mkono wa shati
cutlery	visu na vijiko
earrings	hereni [kipuli/pete yasikio]
hairpin	pini ya nywele
jewel box	boksi la akiba ya dhahabu
manicure set	vifaa vya kukatia kucha
mechanical pencil	penseli ya kujaza
necklace	utepe wa shingoni
pendant	kipuli
pin	pini
powder compact	kiboksi cha podari
propelling pencil	penseli ya kujaza
ring	pete
engagement ring	pete ya uchumba
signet ring	pete yenye muhuri
wedding ring	pete ya arusi
rosary	tasbihi
silverware	vyombo vya fedha
snuff box	boksi la tumbaku
strap	ukanda
chain strap	ukanda wa mnyororo
leather strap	ukanda wa ngozi
watch strap	ukanda wa saa
tie clip	kibano [klipu] cha tai
tie pin	pini ya tai
vanity case	kiboksi cha umalidadi
watch	saa
calendar watch	saa yenye tarehe [na siku]
pocket watch	saa ya mfukoni
with a second hand	yenye mkono wa nukta
wristwatch	saa ya mkono

Laundry—Dry cleaning

If your hotel doesn't have its own laundry or dry cleaning service, ask the porter:

Where's the nearest ...?	Yuko wapi ... aliye karibu?
laundry	dobi [mfua nguo]
dry cleaner s	dobi wa nguo za sufu
I want these clothes ...	Nataka nguo hizi ...
cleaned	zisafishwe
pressed	zipigwe pasi
ironed	zipigwe pasi
washed	zioshwe
I need it ...	Naitaka ...
today	leo
tonight	usiku
tomorrow	kesho
before Friday	kabla ya Ijumaa
I want it as soon as possible.	Naitaka upesi kama inavyomkinika [inavyowezekana].
Can you ... this?	Unaweza kui ... hii?
mend/patch/stitch	-tengeneza/-tia kiraka/-shona
Can you sew on this button?	Unaweza kutia kifungo hiki?
Can you get this stain out?	Unaweza kutoa doa hili?
Can this be invisibly mended?	Yawezekana kuitengeneza hii pasipo kuonekana?
This isn't mine.	Hii siyo yangu.
There's one piece missing.	Nguo moja imepotea
There's a hole in this.	Hii ina tundu.
Is my laundry ready?	Nguo zangu ziko [ni] tayari?

Photography–Cameras

While you're in a tropical climate it's not advisable to leave a film in your camera for a long time. It's worth asking if the films you take with you are suited to hot climates.

Basic still and home-movie exposure instructions are given in English with the information provided with the roll.

I want an inexpensive camera.	**Nataka kamera iliyo rahisi.**
Show me the one in the window.	**Nionyeshe ile iliyopo dirishani.**

Film

I'd like a film for this camera.	**Nataka filimu ya kamera hii.**
I'd like a ... film.	**Nataka filimu ...**
120 (6×6)	**mia moja na ishirini**
127 (4×4)	**mia moja ishirini na saba**
135 (24×36)	**mia moja thelathini na tano**
620 (6×6)	**mia sita na ishirini**
Polaroid	**Polaroidi**
8-mm	**milimita nane**
super 8-mm	**supa milimita nane**
single 8-mm	**singlo milimita nane**
16-mm	**milimita kumi na sita**
620 (6×6) roll	**roli mia sita na ishirini**
20/36 exposures	**eksiposa ishirini/thelathini na sita**
I'd like ...	**Nataka ...**
this ASA/DIN number	**hii ni nambari ya ASA/DIN**
black and white	**filim isiyo na rangi**
colour negative	**filim ya rangi**
colour slide (transparency)	**filim ya slaidi ya rangi**
artificial light type (indoor)	**filim ya kofutoa na taa**
daylight type (outdoor)	**filim ya kufotoa juani**
fast/fine grain	**picha ya mara/muda**
Does the price include processing?	**Bei yake pamoja na kusafisha filim?**

FOR NUMBERS, see page 175

SHOPPING GUIDE

Processing

How much do you charge for developing/printing?	**Bei gani unatoza kwa kusafisha filimu/kufanya picha?**
I want ... prints of each negative.	**Nataka picha ... za kila filimu.**
With a glossy/mat finish.	**Yenye kung'aa/isiyo ng'aa.**
Will you please enlarge this?	**Unaweza kuitanua hii?**
When will it be ready?	**Siku gani itakuwa tayari?**

Accessories

I want a/an/some ...	**Nataka ...**
flash bulbs	**globu za taa ya picha**
flash cubes	**globu za kamera**
for black and white	**za picha bila ya rangi**
for colour	**za picha za rangi**
filter	**filta**
red/yellow	**nyekundu/manjano**
ultra-violet	**marijuani mno**
lens cleaners	**kusafisha lens**

Broken

This camera doesn't work. Can you repair it?	**Kemera hii imeharibika. Unaweza kuitengeneza?**
The film is jammed.	**Filimu imeganda ndani.**
There's something wrong with the ...	**Kuna kitu kilichoharibika katika ...**
exposure counter	**nambari za picha**
film winder	**usukani wa filimu**
flash attachment	**kipandikaji taa**
lens	**lens**
lightmeter	**mita ya jua**
rangefinder	**kioo cha kutazamia**
shutter	**kifungo cha kufotoa**

Provisions

Here is a basic list of food and drink that you might want on a picnic or for the occasional meal at home. It's worth going to the market place for your grocery needs in East Africa. The market usually has separate sections for fish, meat, fruit and vegetables.

I'd like some ...	Nataka ...
apples	matofaa
bananas	ndizi
biscuits	biskuti
bread	mkate
butter	siagi
cake	keki
candy	peremende (tamutamu)
cheese	jibini
chocolate	chakleti
coffee	kahawa [buni]
cold cuts	vipande vya nyama baridi
cookies	biskuti
cooking fat	mafuta ya kupikia
crackers	biskuti za chumvi
cream	krimu ya maziwa
crisps	viazi vya kukaanga vikavu
cucumbers	matango
eggs	mayai
flour	unga
ham	nyama baridi ya nguruwe
hamburgers	hamburger
ice-cream	barafu ya krimu
lemonade	soda ya ndimu
lemons	ndimu
lettuce	figili
liver sausage	soseji ya maini
luncheon meat	nyama ya chakula cha adhuhuri
milk	maziwa
mustard	haradali
oranges	machungwa
pepper	pilipili
pickles	achali
potato chips	viazi vya kukaanga
potatoes	viazi
rolls	mkate wa kusukuma

salad	**saladi**
salt	**chumvi**
sandwiches	**mkate uliojazwa vyakula**
sausages	**soseji**
sugar	**sukari**
sweets	**halua**
tea	**majani ya chai**
tomatoes	**nyanya [tungule]**

And don't forget ...

a bottle opener	**ufunguo wa chupa**
a corkscrew	**ufunguo wa kizibo cha chupa**
matches	**kibiriti**
(paper) napkins	**vianjifu (vya karatasi)**
a tin (can) opener	**ufunguo wa kibati**

Weights and measures

1 kilogram or kilo (kg.) = 1000 grams (g.)

100 g. = 3.5 oz.	¹/₂ kg. = 1.1 lb.
200 g. = 7.0 oz.	1 kg. = 2.2 lb.

1 oz. = 28.35 g.
1 lb. = 453.60 g.

---

1 litre (l.) = 0.88 imp. quarts = 1.06 U.S. quarts

1 imp. quart = 1.14 l.	1 U.S. quart = 0.95 l.
1 imp. gallon = 4.55 l.	1 U.S. gallon = 3.8 l.

---

barrel	**pipa**
box	**boksi**
carton	**kibweta**
crate	**sanduku**
jar	**kasiki [mtungi]**
packet	**pakiti**
tin (can)	**kopo**
tube	**mwanzi**

Souvenirs

East Africa is a shopper's paradise for exotic souvenirs. Items ranging from carved wooden statuettes to leather goods, from seashells to precious stones can be purchased everywhere in town. You'll find merchandise on display outdoors, too—either in front of shop windows or on market stands.

Wood and ivory

carved wooden statuette	**kisanamu cha mti**
ivory statuette	**kisanamu cha pembe**
letter opener	**kisu cha barua**
wooden	**cha mti**
ivory	**cha pembe**
local pipe	**kiko [mtemba]**
with/without filter	**yenye/isio na filta**
wooden elephant	**tembo wa mti**
small/medium/big	**mdogo/kadiri/mkubwa**
with ivory tusks	**mwenye pembe hasa**
wooden ring, engraved	**pete ya mti yenye sura**
with an image	**maarufu**
wooden salad set	**vyombo vya mti vya saladi**

Metal and seashells

copper tray	**sinia ya shaba**
seashells	**kombe za baharini**
silver tray	**sinia ya fedha**
spoon with the name of	**kijiko chenye jina la mahali**
the town	

Stones

precious stone	**jiwe la thamani**
stone for a ring	**jiwe la pete**

Leather and wool

decorative tapestry	**kizulia cha ukutani**
leather purse	**kifuko cha fedha changozi**
tobacco pouch	**mfuko wa tumbaku**
woollen rug	**kizulia cha sufi**
hand-made	**kilichofanywa kwa mkono**

Pottery and straw

demi-tasse with a traditional design	**kikombe kidogo cha kahawa**
straw basket	**mkoba wa ukindi**
straw mat	**busati la ukindi**

Local wearing apparel

Buibui	Black robe worn by Moslim women to hide their beauty from men's attention!
Bunge	A collarless shirt worn also for official functions. Very comfortable in warm climates.
Kofia ya mkono [ya cherehani]	Handmade cap (sometimes machine-made) embroidered in various traditional designs. The price depends on the amount of handwork. Some are very expensive.
Viatu vya makubadhi	Handmade leather sandals; some are colourfully embroidered on the top.
Viatu vya miti [mtalawanda]	Wooden shoes; the elaborate ones have small bells attached to them.

Be on the look-out for locally-made bracelets. Ask for *duka la sonara* (jeweller's) where a variety of designs and types to suit your purse is displayed. Most of these craftsmen can make the design of your choice within one or two days. For a slight surcharge you can also ask the *sonara* to engrave your name on the article you choose.

Another feature of cosmopolitan East Africa is the variety of Indian saris which you can buy. When you do your shopping in the coastal regions you'll easily come across an Oriental goods store.

Don't forget, haggling is customary in East African markets and small shops.

Tobacconist's

As·at home, cigarettes are generally referred to by their brand names. *Mkasi* and *777* are cheap, local brands. Foreign brands manufactured locally are equally inexpensive. Imported cigarettes are heavily taxed and therefore sold at a premium price.

Give me a/an/some ...	Nipe ...
chewing tobacco	mshuku
cigar	sigaa
cigars	sigaa
cigarette case	kisanduku cha kutia sigara
cigarette holder	mwanzi wa kuvutia sigara
cigarette lighter	kibiriti cha mafuta
flints	mawe ya kibiriti
lighter	kibiriti
lighter fluid	mafuta ya kibiriti
lighter gas	gesi ya kibiriti
refill for a lighter	kijazo cha kibiriti
matches	kibiriti
packet of cigarettes	pakti ya sigara
pipe	kiko
pipe cleaners	waya wa kusafisha kiko
pipe tobacco	tumbaku ya kiko
tobacco pouch	kifuko cha tumbaku

Do you have any ...?	Unazo ...?
American cigarettes	sigara za Kimarekani
English cigarettes	sigara za Kiingereza
local cigarettes	sigara za mahali
menthol cigarettes	sigara za nanaa
clove-flavoured cigarettes	sigara za karafuu

I'd like a carton.	Nataka boksi zima.

filter-tipped	zenye filta
king-size	king-size
without filter	pasi na filta

Would you like a cigarette?	Unapenda sigara?
Have one of mine.	Chukua hii yangu.

Your money: banks—currency

At larger banks there's sure to be someone who speaks English. At most tourist resorts you'll find small currency exchanges *(mvunja pesa)* open all the year round.

Hours

Monday to Friday from 8.30 or 9 a.m. to 2 p.m. The currency-exchange offices at major airports are open round the clock every day of the year.

Monetary unit

The basic unit of the East African monetary system is the shilling *(shilingi)* which is divided into 100 cents. The abbreviation for shilling is *Sh.* (derived from the British shilling). Although the rate of exchange of the three East African countries is the same, their shillings aren't interchangeable.

Denomination	Written as
Coins	
Ndururu (5 cents)	–/05
Senti kumi (10 cents)	–/10
Nusu shilingi (1/2 shilling)	–/50
Shilingi moja (1 shilling)	1/00
Notes	
Shilingi tano (5 shillings)	5/00
Shilingi kumi (10 shillings)	10/00
Shilingi ishirini (20 shillings)	20/00
Shilingi hamsini (50 shillings)	50/00
Shilingi mia (100 shillings)	100/00
Shilingi mia mbili (200 shillings)	200/00

Before going

Where's the nearest bank/currency-exchange office?	**Kuna benki/mahali pa kuvunja pesa hapa karibu?**
Where can I cash a traveller's cheque (check)?	**Wapi naweza kuvunja cheki za wasafiri?**

Inside

I want to change some dollars.	**Nataka kuvunja dola za Kimarekani.**
I'd like to change some pounds.	**Nataka kuvunja pauni za Kiingereza.**
Here's my passport.	**Hii paspoti yangu.**
Here's my customs currency declaration.	**Hiki cheti changu cha pesa niliyoingiza.**

Note: In countries where there are currency restrictions you may have to take a copy of your customs declaration with you to the bank.

What's the exchange rate?	**Thamani gani kuvunja pesa hizi?**
What rate of commission do you charge?	**Ujira gani wa kuvunja unalipisha?**
Can you cash a personal cheque?	**Unaweza kuvunja cheki ya binafsi?**
How long will it take to clear?	**Muda gani itachukua kumaliza?**
Can you wire my bank in London?	**Unaweza kumipigia simu kwa benki yangu London?**
I have ...	**Nina ...**
a letter of credit an introduction from ... a credit card	**barua ya credit kijulisho kutoka kwa ... kadi ya credit**

I'm expecting some money from Manchester. Has it arrived yet?	**Nataraji pesa kutoka Manchester. Zimefika au bado?**
Please give me ... notes (bills) and some small change.	**Tafadhali nipe ... noti na pesa ndogo.**
Give me ... large notes and the rest in small notes.	**Nipe noti kubwa ... na zilobaki noti ndogo.**
Could you please check that again?	**Tafadhali unaweza kuhesabu hizo tena?**

Depositing

I want to credit this to my account.	**Nataka kutia hii katika hesabu yangu.**
I want to credit this to Mr ...'s account.	**Nataka kutia hii katika hesabu ya Bwana ...**
Where should I sign?	**Wapi nitie sahihi?**

Currency converter

In a world of floating currencies, we can offer no more than this do-it-yourself chart. You can get a card showing current exchange rates from banks, travel agents and tourist offices. Why not fill in this chart, too, for handy reference?

Sh.	£	$
–/10 cents		
–/50 cents		
1 shilling		
5 shillings		
10 shillings		
50 shillings		
100 shillings		
500 shillings		
1000 shillings		
5000 shillings		

FOR NUMBERS, see page 175

At the post office

Post offices are indicated by the letters PTT (Post, Telephone and Telegraph). Mailboxes are painted red. Business hours are from 8 a.m. to noon and from 2 to 4.30 p.m.

Can you tell me how to get to the post office?	**Unaweza kunionyesha njia ya kwenda posta?**
What time does the post office open/close?	**Saa ngapi inafunguliwa/inafungwa posta?**
What window do I go to for stamps?	**Niende dirisha gani kununua stempu?**
At which counter can I cash an international money order?	**Mahali gani naweza kuvunja cheti cha pesa cha ulimwengu?**
I want some stamps.	**Nataka stempu.**
I want ... 30-cent stamps and ... 50-cent stamps.	**Nataka stempu ... za senti 30 na ... za nusu shilingi.**
What's the postage for an airmail letter to London?	**Kiasi gani kutuma barua London kwa ndege?**
What's the postage for an airmail postcard to Los Angeles?	**Kiasi gani kutuma kadi ya posta Los Angeles kwa ndege?**
aerogramme	**barua ya ndege**
surface mail	**barua isiyo ya ndege**
When (approximately) will this letter get there?	**(Kama) siku gani itafika barua hii?**
Give me an airmail label.	**Nipe kipande [label] cha barua ya ndege.**

Note: You can also buy stamps at stationers', souvenir shops or small grocers' in East Africa.

I want to send this parcel.	**Nataka kutuma bahasha hii.**
Do I have to fill in a customs declaration?	**Itabidi nijaze cheti cha kastamu?**
I want to register this letter.	**Nataka kurejista barua hii.**
Where s the mailbox?	**Wapi sanduku la kutia barua?**
airmail	**kwa ndege**
express (special delivery)	**ya haraka**
registered mail	**barua ya rejista**
Where's the post restante (general delivery)?	**Wapi mahali pa kupokea barua zijazo?**
Is there any mail for me? My name's ...	**Ipo barua yangu? Jina langu ni ...**

STEMPU	STAMPS
BAHASHA	PARCELS
UTUMISHI WA PESA	MONEY ORDERS

Cables (telegrams)

Where's the (nearest) telegraph office?	**Wapi ofisi ya kupeleka simu za nje (iliyo karibu)?**
I want to send a telegram. May I please have a form?	**Nataka kutuma simu. Unaweza kunipa fomu za maneno?**
How much is it per word?	**Kiasi gani kwa kila neno?**
How long will a cable to Boston take?	**Muda gani itachukua simu kwenda Boston?**
I'd like to reverse the charges.	**Nataka gharama za simu zilipwe na mpokeaji.**
What's the maximum number of words for a night-rate telegram (night letter)?	**Itabidi maneno mangapi kwa simu ya LT?**

Telephoning

The telephone system in East Africa is operated as a joint service of Kenya, Tanzania and Uganda and you can dial directly to any one of these countries with the correct dialling (area) code. To call long distance outside East Africa, you'll have to place the call through the operator.

Where's the telephone?	**Ipo wapi simu?**
Where's the nearest telephone booth?	**Wapi kijumba cha simu kilichopo karibu?**
May I use your phone?	**Naweza kutumia simu yako?**
Do you have a telephone directory for Kampala?	**Unayo orodha ya nambari za simu za Kampala?**
Can you help me get this number?	**Unaweza kunisaidia kutafuta nambari hii?**

Note: In the absence of a telephone booth, you can make your call from any shop or restaurant.

Operator

Do you speak English?	**Unasema Kiingereza?**
Good morning, I want Mombasa 12345.	**Habari za asubuhi, Nataka Mombasa 12345.**
Can I dial direct?	**Naweza kupiga simu moja kwa moja?**
I want to place a personal (person to person) call.	**Nataka kupiga simu kwa mtu hasa ninayemtaka.**
I want to reverse the charges (call collect).	**Nataka gharama za simu zilipwe na mpokeaji.**
Will you tell me the cost of the call afterwards?	**Niarifu gharama za pigo la simu hii baadaye.**

FOR NUMBERS, see page 175

Speaking

Hello. This is ... speaking.	**Hallo. Mimi ... ninayesema.**
I want to speak to ...	**Nataka kusema na ...**
Would you put me through to ...?	**Unaweza kunipa ...?**
I want extension ...	**Nataka simu ya ndani ...**
Is that ...?	**Eti huyo ...?**

Bad luck

Would you please try again later?	**Unapenda kujaribu mara nyingine baadaye?**
Operator, you gave me the wrong number.	**Opereta, umenipa nambari isiyo sawa.**
Operator, we were cut off.	**Opereta, tumekatiwa simu.**

Telephone alphabet

A	Aali		N	Nairobi
B	Bibi		O	Olga
C	Cyprus		P	Paul
D	Daniel		Q	Quebec
E	Elfu		R	Robert
F	Fiwi		S	Sana
G	Gombe		T	Tanga
H	Henry		U	Unga
I	Ida		V	Victor
J	Jinja		W	William
K	Kenya		X	Xavier
L	Leso		Y	Yatima
M	Mtu		Z	Zanzibar

Not there

When will he/she be back?	**Lini atarudi?**
Will you tell him/her I called? My name's ...	**Muarifu nimepiga simu. Jina langu ...**
Would you ask him/her to call me?	**Muarifu anipigie simu.**
Would you please take a message?	**Unaweza kuchukua maagizo?**

Charges

What was the cost of that call?	**Ilikura [Gharama] gani ya simu ile?**
I want to pay for the call.	**Nataka kulipa hesabu ya simu.**

Kuna simu kwa ajili yako.	There's a telephone call for you.
Subiri kidogo.	Please hold the line.
Unasema kutoka nambari gani?	What number are you calling?
Simu ina shughuli.	The line's engaged.
Hapana jawabu.	There's no answer.
Umepata nambari isiyo sawa.	You've got the wrong number.
Hayupo sasa.	He's/She's out at the moment.

The car

We'll start this section by considering your possible needs at a filling station. Most of them don't handle major repairs; but apart from providing you with fuel, they may be helpful in solving all kinds of minor problems.

Where's the nearest filling (service) station?	**Wapi kituo cha petroli kilicho karibu?**
I want 20 litres of petrol (gas), please.	**Nataka lita 20, tafadhali.**
I want 30 litres of standard/premium.	**Nataka lita 30 za standardi/premium.**
Give me 40 shillings worth of ...	**Nipe ... ya kadiri ya shilingi 40.**
Fill 'er up, please.	**Tafadhali jaza tanki.**
Please check the oil and water.	**Tafadhali angalia mafuta na maji.**
Give me 2 litres of oil.	**Nipe lita 2 za mafuta.**
Fill up the battery with distilled water.	**Jaza betri na maji ya distil.**

Fluid measures					
litres	imp. gal.	US. gal.	litres	imp. gal.	US. gal.
5	1.1	1.3	30	6.6	7.8
10	2.2	2.6	35	7.7	9.1
15	3.3	3.9	40	8.8	10.4
20	4.4	5.2	45	9.9	11.7
25	5.5	6.5	50	11.0	13.0

FOR NUMBERS, see page 175

	Check the brake fluid.	**Angalia mafuta ya breki.**

Would you check the tire pressure? — **Angalia mipira.**

1.6 front, 1.8 rear. — **Nambari 1 pointi 6 mbele, 1 pointi 8 nyuma.**

Tire pressure			
lb./sq. in.	kg./cm.^{2}	lb./sq. in.	kg./cm.^{2}
10	0.7	26	1.8
12	0.8	27	1.9
15	1.1	28	2.0
18	1.3	30	2.1
20	1.4	33	2.3
21	1.5	36	2.5
23	1.6	38	2.7
24	1.7	40	2.8

Please check the spare tire, too. — **Tafadhali angalia mpira wa speya pia.**

Can you mend this puncture (fix this flat)? — **Unaweza kuiziba pancha hii?**

Would you please change this tire? — **Unaweza kubadilisha mpira huu?**

Would you clean the windscreen (windshield)? — **Unaweza kusafisha kioo cha gari?**

Have you a road map of this district? — **Unayo ramani ya mtaa huu?**

Where are the toilets? — **Kipo wapi choo?**

CAR—FILLING STATION

Asking the way—Street directions

Excuse me.	**Samahani.**
Can you tell me the way to …?	**Unaweza kunionesha njia ya kwenda …?**
How do I get to …?	**Vipi kwenda …?**
Where does this road lead to?	**Njia hii inafika [inakwenda] wapi?**
Are we on the right road for …?	**Tuko katika njia sawasawa ya kwenda …?**
How far is the next village?	**Umbali gani mtaa wa pili?**
How far is it to … from here?	**Umbali gani kwenda … kutoka hapa?**
Can you tell me where … is?	**Unaweza kuniambia ni wapi …?**
Where can I find this address?	**Wapi ninaweza kupata anwani hii?**
Where's this?	**Hapa ni wapi?**

Miles into kilometres									
1 mile = 1.609 kilometres (km.)									
miles	10	20	30	40	50	60	70	80	90	100
km.	16	32	48	64	80	97	113	129	145	161

Kilometres into miles												
1 kilometre (km.) = 0.62 miles												
km.	10	20	30	40	50	60	70	80	90	100	110	120	130
miles	6	12	19	25	31	37	44	50	56	62	68	75	81

Can you show me on the map where I am?	**Unaweza kunionyesha kwenye ramani hii mahali nilipo?**
Can you show me on the map where the university is?	**Unaweza kunionyesha katika ramani chuo kikuu kiko wapi?**
Can I park there?	**Ninaweza kuweka gari langu pale?**
Is that a one way-street?	**Ile ni barabara ya upande mmoja?**
Does the traffic go this way?	**Magari huenda njia hii?**

Umekosea njia.	You're on the wrong road.
Nenda moja kwa moja.	Go straight ahead.
Pale kisha pinda ...	It's down there on the ...
kushoto/kulia	left/right
Nenda mpaka njia panda ya kwanza/ya pili.	Go to the first/second crossroads.
Pinda kushoto penye taa za magari.	Turn left at the traffic lights.
Pinda kulia kwenye mkato wa pili.	Turn right at the next corner.

CAR – FILLING STATION

In the rest of this section we'll be more closely concerned with the car itself. We've divided it into two parts:

Part A contains general advice on motoring in East Africa. It's essentially for reference, and is therefore to be browsed over, preferably in advance.

Part B is concerned with the practical details of accidents and breakdown. It includes a list of car parts and a list of things that may go wrong with them. All you have to do is to show it to the garage mechanic and get him to point to the items required.

Part A

Customs—Documentation

You'll require the following documents:

passport
international insurance certificate
car registration certificate
valid international driving licence

The nationality plate or sticker must be on the car.

In East Africa, you can drive with a British or American driving licence. But if you plan to visit other countries, check whether an international licence is required.

It's rather unlikely that you'll ship your car to East Africa, but if you do it would be wise to check beforehand how long you are allowed to use it in each country without having to pay import duty. Have it cleared by customs as soon as it arrives, otherwise you'll have heavy storage charges to pay.

Here's my ...	Hii ... yangu.
customs pass	cheti cha kastamu
driving licence	leseni ya kuendesha
green card	kadi ya kijani
passport	paspoti

I've nothing to declare.	Sina kitu chochote cha kutozwa ushuru.

I've ...	Nina ...
a carton of cigarettes	boksi la sigara
a bottle of whisky	chupa ya wiski
a bottle of wine	chupa ya divai

We're staying for ...	Tutakaa kwa muda wa ...
a week	wiki moja
two weeks	wiki mbili
a month	mwezi mmoja

CAR – INFORMATION

Driving

East African road construction has yet to catch up with growing traffic demands. Roads in Kenya and Uganda can give you a rather bouncy ride. Zanzibar has good roads over practically the whole island. The road from Dar es Salaam to Tanga and Morogoro is rather rough and pitted, as is the whole stretch of the road from Nairobi to the coastal city of Mombasa in Kenya.

Please note that most of the roads consist merely of a single strip of asphalt—just wide enough to accommodate one vehicle—which fades out into the unimproved adjoining earth. Consequently, it's dangerous, if not impossible to overtake (pass). Also, beware of getting out of your car in the open country; not because of the danger of being mugged by a prowling gangster, but because there is always a slight risk you may be attacked by a wild animal ... Beware of the rhinoceros!

As an inheritance of their British past, the three East African countries drive on the left and overtake on the right. Consequently, the rule is for vehicles to have the steering wheel on the right. However, cars with the steering wheel on the left (as often in the case of tourist-imported cars) are tolerated for the short periods usually involved.

Before driving long distances enquire first at your hotel if the roads are good. Due to the torrential rains which occur at certain times of the year, flooding sometimes cuts the roads completely. Since the rainy season varies according to the area you are in, it's difficult to state here exactly when you might meet these conditions.

The coming years will see a great improvement in road conditions generally, as a result of the vigourous road-building campaigns planned or already in progress.

A special word about driving in the national parks: here speeds are strictly limited to 30 or even 20 miles per hour, so as not to scare off the very wild animals which you are coming to see. For the same reason all loud noises and brusque movements should be avoided, both when driving and while taking photographs.

It's always advisable, and sometimes compulsory, to engage the services of a scout or ranger to accompany you. He will be of invaluable help in the more remote areas of the national parks in piloting you round obstacles and in actually getting you within photographing distance of the big game.

Don't be surprised if you suddenly find your way blocked by several hundredweight of lions or rhinoceros sprawling astride your track. And don't try to nudge them out of the way. Just enjoy the occasion and wait for the animals to move on.

Traffic offences

The police can fine you on the spot. A minor fine must be mailed promptly to or paid at the traffic office. You can opt to go before a local traffic court, but this can be time consuming.

In case of serious trouble, insist on an interpreter.

I'm sorry, Officer. I didn't see the sign.	**Nisamehe, bwana. Sikuona alama.**
I didn't realize my speed.	**Sikutambua kuwa nilienda mbio sana.**
The light was green.	**Taa ilikuwa kijani.**
I'm sorry, I don't speak Swahili.	**Nasikitika, siongei Kiswahili.**
I don't understand.	**Sielewi.**
How much is the fine?	**Faini ni kiasi gani?**

Parking

Use your common sense when parking. The police are normally lenient with tourists but don't push your luck too far.

Comply with the parking regulations which will be indicated by signs or by lines painted on the pavement. In many cities in East Africa, you may park your car on the kerb (curb), even in downtown areas.

Excuse me. May I park here?	**Samahani. Naweza kuweka gari hapa?**
How long may I park here?	**Muda gani naweza kuweka gari hapa?**
What's the charge for parking here?	**Gharama ya kuweka gari hapa ni nini?**
Do I have to leave my lights on?	**Lazima niache taa zangu zikiwaka?**

Part B

Accidents

This section is confined to immediate aid. The legal problems of responsibility and settlement can be taken care of at a later stage.

Your first concern will be for the injured.

Is anyone hurt?	**Kuna mtu aliyeumia?**
Don't move.	**Usisimame.**
It's all right. Don't worry.	**Usiwe na wasiwasi. Hapana jambo.**
Where's the nearest telephone?	**Ipo wapi simu hapa karibu?**
Can I use your telephone? There's been an accident.	**Naweza kutumia simu yako? Kumetokea ajali.**
Call a doctor/an ambulance quickly.	**Mwite daktari/gari la hospitali haraka.**
There are people injured.	**Kuna watu walioumia.**
Help me get them out of the car.	**Nisaidie kuwatoa garini.**

Police – Exchange of information

Please call the police.	**Tafadhali haraka ita polisi.**
There's been an accident. It's about 1 kilometre from ...	**Kumetokea ajali. Kadiri ya kilometa 1 kutoka ...**
I'm on the Mombasa-Malindi road, 12 kilometres from Mombasa.	**Nipo katika barabara ya Mombasa na Malindi. Kilometa 12 kukota Mombasa.**
Here's my name and address.	**Hili jina na anuani yangu.**

CAR – INFORMATION

Would you mind acting as a witness?	**Unajali kuwa shahidi?**
I'd like an interpreter.	**Nataka mkalimani.**

Remember to put out a red triangle warning sign if the car is out of action or impeding traffic.

Breakdown

...and that's what we'll do in this section: break it down into four phases.

1. *On the road*
   You ask where the nearest garage is.

2. *At the garage*
   You tell the mechanic what's wrong.

3. *Finding the trouble*
   He tells you what he thinks is wrong.

4. *Getting it repaired*
   You tell him to repair it and, once that lot is over, settle the account (or argue about it).

Phase 1 – On the road

Where's the nearest garage?	**Wapi gereji iliyo karibu?**
Excuse me. My car has broken down. May I use your phone?	**Samahani. Gari yangu imeharibika. Naweza kutumia simu yako?**
What's the telephone number of the nearest garage?	**Nambari ngapi simu ya gereji iliyo karibu?**
I've had a breakdown at ...	**Imeniharibikia nilipokuwa ...**
We are on the Kampala-Jinja road, about 6 kilometres from Kampala.	**Tupo katika barabara ya Kampala na Jinja, kadiri ya kilometa 6 kukota Kampala.**

The car is a short/long distance away. We are at a shop in ...	**Gari ipo mbali kidogo/ sana. Sisi tupo dukani hapa ...**
Can you send a mechanic?	**Unaweza kuniletea fundi?**
Can you send a truck to tow my car?	**Unaweza kuleta lori livute gari yangu?**
How long will you be?	**Utachukua muda gani?**

Phase 2 – At the garage

Can you help me?	**Unaweza kunisaidia?**
Are you the mechanic?	**Wewe ni fundi wa magari?**
I don't know what's wrong with it.	**Sijui kitu gani kimeharibika.**
I think there's something wrong with the ...	**Nafikiri kuna kitu kilichoharibika katika ...**
battery	**beteri**
brakes	**breki**
bulbs	**taa**
carburettor	**kabureta**
clutch	**klachi**
cooling system	**chombo cha kupooza**
contact	**kontakt**
dimmers, dip switch	**swichi**
dynamo	**dynamo**
electrical system	**chombo cha umeme**
engine	**injini [mtambo]**
exhaust line/pipe	**ekzosi/bomba la ekzosi**
fan	**pepeo**
filter	**filta**
fuel pump/tank	**bomba/tangi la petroli**
gears	**gia**
generator	**dynamo**
hand brake	**breki ya mkono**
headlights	**taa kubwa za gari**
heating	**chombo cha joto**
horn	**honi**
ignition system	**swichi ya stati**

CAR – REPAIRS

indicator	taa za kupindia
lights	taa
backup lights	taa za kuendesha nyuma
brake lights	taa za breki
rear lights	taa za nyuma
reversing lights	taa za kuendeshea nyuma
tail lights	taa za nyuma
lines	waya
lining and covering	kitambaa cha ndani na nje
lubrication system	ujazaji wa mafuta
parking brake	breki ya mkono
radiator	redieta [chombo cha kupoza joto]
reflectors	riflecta
seat	kiti
sliding roof	kipaa cha kufunguka
sparking plugs	spaki
speedometer	mtambo wa spidi [chombo cha kupima mwendo]
starter	stati
steering	usukani
suspension	springi
(automatic) transmission	transmishan (ya otomatik)
turn signals	taa za kupindia
wheels	magurudumu
wipers	vyombo vya kufuta maji

KULIA	KUSHOTO
RIGHT	LEFT

MBELE	NYUMA
FRONT	BACK

It's ...	Ni [Ina] ...
bad	mbovu
blowing	ina shindo
blown	imepasuka
broken	imevunjika
burnt	imeungua
cracked	ina ufa
defective	ina ubovu
disconnected	imeachana
dry	kavu
frozen	ina baridi
jammed	imeganda
knocking	inagonga

CAR – REPAIRS

leaking	**inavuja**
loose	**ina pwaya**
misfiring	**kaishiki moto**
noisy	**ina kelele**
not working	**haifanyi kazi**
overheating	**i moto sana**
short-circuiting	**inagusana moto**
slack	**imelegea**
slipping	**inaponyoka**
stuck	**imekaza**
vibrating	**inatikisika**
weak	**dhaifu**
worn	**imetumika sana**

The car won't start.	**Gari haishiki moto.**
It's locked and the keys are inside.	**Imefungwa na funguo zimo ndani.**
The fan belt is too slack.	**Ukanda wa panka umelegea sana.**
The radiator is leaking.	**Chombo cha kupoza joto kinatoja.**
I want maintenance and lubrication service.	**Nataka usafishaji na kujaza mafuta.**
The idling needs adjusting.	**Mwendo wa injini unahitaji kurekibishwa.**
The clutch engages too quickly.	**Klachi inakamata kwa haraka mno.**
The steering wheel's vibrating.	**Usukani una tikisika.**
The wipers are smearing.	**Vyombo vya kufuta maji vina tia doa.**
The pneumatic suspension is weak.	**Springi za upepo ni dhaifu.**
The ... needs adjusting.	**... inahitaji kurekibishwa.**
brakes/clutch	**breki/klachi**

Now that you've explained what's wrong, you'll want to know how long it'll take to repair it and make your arrangements accordingly.

How long will it take to repair?	**Muda gani itachukua kuitengeneza?**
Suppose I come back in half an hour/tomorrow?	**Jee, kama nikirejea, baada ya nusu saa/kesho?**
Can you give me a lift into town?	**Unaweza kunipeleka mjini?**
Is there a place to stay nearby?	**Hapa karibu kuna mahali pa kukaa?**
May I use your phone?	**Naweza kutumia simu yako?**

Phase 3 – Finding the trouble

It's up to the mechanic either to find the trouble or to repair it. All you have to do is hand him the book and point to the text in Swahili below.

Tafadhali angalia orodha ya alfabeti ifuatayo na onyesha kitu kilichoharibika. Ikiwa mnunuzi wako anahitaji kujua nini hasa imeharibika, onyesha tamko linalofaa katika orodha ijao (imevunjika, imeshikano moto, n.z.).*

CAR – REPAIRS

bering	bearing
beteri	battery
bloki	block
bol bering	main bearings
bomba	pump
bomba la mafuta	oil pump
bomba la maji	water pump
bomba la petroli	petrol pump
bomba la sindano	injection pump
brashi	brushes
breki	brake
chelezo	float
chombo cha kupooza	cooling system
chombo cha mvuke	thermostat
diaphragm	diaphragm
distributa	distributor

* Please look at the following alphabetical list and point to the defective item. If your customer wants to know what is wrong with it, pick the applicable term from the next list (broken, short-circuited, etc.).

dynamo	dynamo (generator)
fen	fan
filta	filter
filta la mafuta	oil filter
filta ya petroli	petrol filter
filta ya upepo	air filter
floti	float
gasket ya kichwa cha silinda	cylinder head gasket
genereta	generator
gia	gear
gurudumu la spidi	tappets
gurudumu la stati	starter motor
imara	stabilizer
injini	engine
jointi	joint
jointi ya gurudumu	universal joint
kabureta	carburettor
kamshafti	camshaft
kichwa cha silinda	cylinder head
kigawanyisha moto	distributor
kipindo	track-rod ends
kiwambo	diaphragm
klachi	clutch
koil	ignition oil
kondensa	condensor
kontakt	contact
krankes	crank-case
krankshaft	crankshaft
lining	lining
magurudumu	wheels
maji ya beteri	battery liquid
maji yaliochemshwa	distilled water
mawe ya beteri	battery cells
meno ya gurudumu	teeth
mguu wa klachi	clutch pedal
mpira wa breki	brake drum
mshikano	connection
nguzo ya usukani	steering column
pepeo	fan
pete za gari	rings
pete za piston	piston rings
piston	piston
point	points
redieta	radiator
reki na pinion	rack and pinion

sahani ya klachi	clutch plate
sanduku la gia	gear box
sanduku la usukani	steering box
saspenshan	suspension
shafti	shaft
shahamu ya gari	grease
shokomzoba	shock-absorber
silinda	cylinder
spaki	sparking plugs
springi	springs
springi ya valvu	valve spring
springi za kuelea	pressure springs
springi za upepo	pneumatic suspension
stabalaiza	stabilizer
stati	starter armature
stemu	stems
swichi ya taa	dip switch (dimmer switch)
transmishan	transmission
transmishan ya otomatik	automatic transmission
ukanda wa panka	fan-belt
umeme	electrical system
usukani	steering
valvu	valve
viatu vya injini	shoes
vichwa vya distributa	distributor leads
vichwa vya spaki	sparking-plug leads
waya	cable

Orodha ifuatayo inayo maneno yanayoeleza vitu visivyosawa na pia vile vinavyohitaji kutengenezwa (katika gari).*

chafu	dirty
chini	low
dhaifu	weak
fanya rilain	to reline
fupi	short
haiwashi	misfiring
ifungue	to loosen
imeachana	disconnected
imeganda	jammed
imeganda na baridi	frozen

*The following list contains words which describe what's wrong as well as what may need to be done.

imevunjika	warped
imelegea	slack
imepasuka	blown
imesakama	stuck
imetumika sana	worn
imeungua	burnt
i moto sana	overheating
inacheza	play
inagonga	knocking
ina pancha	punctured
ina kutu	corroded
ina mbio	quick
inapwaya	loose
inateleza	slipping
inatikisika	vibrating
inatoja	leaking
ina ufa	cracked
juu	high
kavu	dry
kubadilisha	to replace/to change
kuchaji	to charge
kufyota	to bleed
kukaza	to tighten
kupasua	blowing
kurekibisha	to adjust
kusafisha	to clean
kusaga ndani	to grind in
kusawazisha	to balance
mbovu	defective
umetoboka	punctured
waya zinashikana	short-circuited

Phase 4 – Getting it repaired

Have you found the trouble? **Umeona nini imeharibika?**

Now that you know what's wrong, or at least have some idea, you'll want to find out...

Is that serious?	**Je hiyo muhimu?**
Can you repair it?	**Unaweza kuitengeneza?**
What's it going to cost?	**Gharama yake itakuwa nini?**
Do you have the necessary spare parts?	**Unavyo vyombo vinavyohitaji kubadilishwa?**

What if he says "no"?

Why can't you do it?	**Kwa nini huwezi kuifanya?**
Is it essential to have that part?	**Kwani lazima kupata chombo hicho?**
How long is it going to take to get the spare part?	**Muda gani itachukua kupata chombo kipya?**
Where's the nearest garage that can repair it?	**Wapi gereji iliyo karibu itakayoweza kuitengeneza?**
Can you fix it so that I can get as far as ...?	**Unaweza kuitengeneza ili [hata] niweze kwenda mpaka ...?**

If you're really stuck, ask if you can leave the car at the garage. Check with the garage if you can hire another car.

Can I leave the car here?	**Naweza kuiacha gari hapa?**
Can I hire another car from you/your garage?	**Naweza kukodi gari nyingine kutoka kwako/gereji yako?**

Settling the bill

Is everything fixed?	**Yote imetengenezwa?**
How much do I owe you?	**Kiasi gani nilipe?**
Will you take a travellers cheque?	**Unachukua malipo kwa cheki za wasafiri?**
Thanks very much for your help.	**Asante sana kwa msaada wako.**
This is for you.	**Hii kwa ajili yako.**

But you may feel that the workmanship is sloppy or that you're paying for work not done. Get the bill itemized. If necessary, get it translated before you pay.

I'll like to check the bill first. Will you itemize the work done?	**Nataka kusahihisha hesabu kwanza. Nipe hesabu ya kila kitu, ya kazi iliyofanya.**

If the garage still won't back down and you're sure you're right, it may be enough to indicate your intention to call a third party.

Some East African road signs

One way

No entry

NO STOPPING

No parking

End of restriction

Yield right of way

Caution

Series of bends (curves)

Intersection with secondary road

No through road

Hospital zone

161

 Crossroads (intersection)

 Unguarded level (railroad) crossing

 Road narrows

 Uneven road (bumps)

 Bend (curve)

 Side road

 Steep hill

 Roundabout (rotary)

 Children's crossing

 Cattle crossing

 Double bend (curve)

 No overtaking (passing)

 YIELD

 STOP

 Speed limit in miles

 Main road (thoroughfare)

Doctor

Frankly, how much use is a phrase book going to be to you in case of serious injury or illness? The only phrase you need in such an emergency is …

Get a doctor quickly!	**Mwite daktari haraka!**

But there are minor aches and pains, ailments and irritations that can upset the best planned trip. Here we can help you and, perhaps, the doctor.

Some doctors will speak English well; others will know enough for your needs. But suppose there's something the doctor can't explain because of language difficulties? We've thought of that. As you'll see, this section has been arranged to enable you and the doctor to communicate. From pages 165 to 171, you find your part of the dialogue on the upper half of each page— the doctor's is on the lower half.

The whole section has been divided into three parts: illness, wounds, nervous tension. Page 171 is concerned with prescriptions and fees.

General

I need a doctor quickly.	**Nahitaji daktari haraka.**
Can you get me a doctor?	**Unaweza kuniitia daktari?**
Is there a doctor here?	**Yupo daktari hapa?**
Please telephone for a doctor immediately.	**Tafadhali mpigie simu daktari sasa hivi.**
Where is there a doctor who speaks English?	**Yupo wapi daktari anaye-sema Kiingereza?**

Is there an English/American hospital in town?	Ipo hospitali ya Kiingereza/Kimarekani hapa mjini?
Where's the surgery (doctor's office)?	Kipo wapi chumba cha daktari?
Could the doctor come to see me here?	Daktari anaweza kuja kunitazema hapa?
What time can the doctor come?	Saa ngapi anaweza kuja daktari?

Symptoms

Use this section to tell the doctor what's wrong. Basically, what he'll require to know is:

What?   (ache, pain, bruise, etc.)
Where?   (arm, stomach, etc.)
How long? (have you had the trouble)

Before you visit the doctor find out the answers to these questions by glancing through the pages that follow. In this way, you'll save time.

Parts of the body

ankle	kifundo cha mguu
appendix	chango
arm	mkono
artery	mshipa wa damu
back	mgongo
bladder	kibofu
blood	damu
bone	mfupa
bowels	matumbo
breast	matiti
cheek	shavu
chest	kifua
chin	kidevu
collar-bone	mtulinga
ear	sikio
elbow	kiko cha mkono

DOCTOR

eye	jicho
face	uso
finger	kidole
foot	mguu
forehead	paji la uso
gland	mtoki
hair	nywele
hand	mkono
head	kichwa
heart	moyo
heel	kisigino
hip	nyonga
intestines	utumbo
jaw	utaya
joint	kiungo
kidney	figo
knee	goti
knee cap	fuu la goti
leg	mguu
liver	maini
lung	pafu
mouth	mdomo
muscle	musuli
neck	shingo
nerve	mshipa wa fahamu
nose	pua
rib	ubavu
shoulder	bega
skin	ngozi
spine	uti wa mgongo
stomach	tumbo
tendon	ukano
thigh	paja
throat	koo
thumb	kidole gumba
toe	kidole cha mguu
tongue	ulimi
tonsils	kilimi [tonseli]
urine	mkojo
vein	mshipa
waist	kiuno
wrist	kifundo cha mkono

PATIENT

Part 1 — Illness

I'm not feeling well.	**Sijisikii vizuri.**
I'm ill.	**Ni mgonjwa [Siwezi].**
I've got a pain here.	**Hapa panauma.**
His/Her ... hurts.	**... yake inauma.**
I've got (a) ...	**Naumwa na ...**
headache/backache	**kichwa/mgongo**
fever/sore throat	**homa/banguzi kooni**
travel sickness	**ugonjwa wa safari**
I'm constipated.	**Sipati choo.**
I've been vomiting.	**Ninatapika.**

DOCTOR

Sehem 1 — Ugonjwa

Wapi panauma?	Where does it hurt?
Una nini?	What's the trouble?
Muda gani umeumwa hapa?	How long have you had this pain?
Kwa muda gani umehisi namna hivi?	How long have you been feeling like this?
Pandisha mkono wa shati.	Roll up your sleeve.
Vua suruali yako na andawia.	Please remove your trousers and underpants.
Vua nguo zako (mpaka kiunoni).	Please undress (down to the waist).

DOCTOR

PATIENT

I feel ...	Nahisi ...
faint/dizzy	machofu/kizunguzungu
nauseous/shivery	kuchafuka moyo/kutetemeka
abcess	jipu
asthma	pumu
boil	jipu
chill	baridi
cold	kamasi [mafua]
constipation	kufunga choo
convulsions	kifafa
children's convulsions	dege
cramps	kiharusi
diarrhoea	kuhara
fever	homa
haemorrhoids	buasiri
hay fever	homa ya makamasi

DOCTOR

Lala hapa.	Please lie down over here.
Fungua mdomo wako.	Open your mouth.
Vuta pumzi kwa nguvu.	Breathe deeply.
Kohoa.	Cough, please.
Nitapima homa yako.	I'll take your temperature.
Nitapima nguvu za damu yako.	I'm going to take your blood pressure.
Hii ni mara ya kwanza kupata ugonjwa huu?	Is this the first time you've had this?
Nitakupiga sindano.	I'll give you an injection.
Nataka sehemu ya mkojo/choo wako.	I want a specimen of your urine/stools.

DOCTOR

PATIENT

hernia	**mshipa**
indigestion	**kuvimbiwa na tumbo**
inflammation of ...	**mchomo wa ...**
influenza	**homa ya mafua**
morning sickness	**udhaifu wa asubuhi**
rheumatism	**baridi yabisi**
stiff neck	**shingo imekazana**
sunburn	**kuungua na jua**
sunstroke	**kuchomwa na jua**
tonsillitis	**tonsili**
ulcer	**kidonda cha tumboni**
whooping cough	**kifaduro**

It's nothing serious, I hope?	**Hakuna kitu kibaya natumaini?**
I'd like you to prescribe some medicine for me.	**Nataka uniandikie dawa.**

DOCTOR

Hapana jambo la kuhangaisha.	It's nothing to worry about.
Lazima upumzike kitandani kwa muda wa siku ...	You must stay in bed for ... days
Una ...	You've got ...
yabisi kavu	arthritis
homa ya mapafu	pneumonia
homa ya mafua	an influenza
chakula kilichooza	food poisoning
mchomo wa ...	an inflammation of ...
jipu la tumboni	an appendicitis
Unavuta sigara/unalewa bila ya kadiri.	You're smoking/drinking too much.
Umechoka zaidi. Unahitaji kupumzika.	You're over-tired. You need a rest.
Nataka uende hospitali ukatazamwe zaidi.	I want you to go to the hospital for a general check-up.
Nitakuandikia sumu ya vidudu.	I'll prescribe an antibiotic.

DOCTOR

PATIENT

I'm a diabetic.	**Mimi nina ugonjwa wa kisukari.**
I've a cardiac condition.	**Nina ugonjwa wa moyo.**
I had a heart attack in ...	**Nilipata mpigo wa moyo katika ...**
I'm allergic to ...	**Sipatani na ...**
This is my usual medicine.	**Hii ni dawa yangu ya desturi.**
I need this medicine.	**Nahitaji dawa hii.**
I'm expecting a baby.	**Ni mja mzito.**
Can I travel?	**Naweza kusafiri?**

DOCTOR

Aina gani ya insulin unachukua?	What dose of insulin are you taking?
Sindano au dawa ya kunywa?	Injection or oral?
Umepata utibabu namna gani?	What treatment have you been having?
Aina gani ya dawa unatumia?	What medicine have you been taking?
Umepata mpigo wa moyo (kidogo).	You've had a (slight) heart attack.
Hatutumii ... hapa Kenya. Hii haina tofauti yoyote.	We don't use ... in Kenya. This is very similar.
Unatazamia kupata mtoto lini?	When's the baby due?
Huwezi kusafiri mpaka ...	You can't travel until ...

PATIENT

Part 2 — Wounds

Could you have a look at this ...?	**Unaweza kunitazama ... hili?**
blister	**lengelenge**
boil	**jipu**
bruise	**chubuko**
burn	**kuungua moto**
cut	**jeraha**
graze	**mparuzo**
insect bite	**kutafunwa na mdudu**
lump	**kifungu**
rash	**kipele**
sting	**mwiba**
swelling	**uvimbe**
wound	**jeraha [kidonda]**

DOCTOR

Sehem 2 — Majeraha

Imeambukizwa/ Haikuambukizwa.	It's infected/ It isn't infected.
Umeteguka uti wa mgongo.	You've got a slipped disc.
Nataka ukafanye X-ray.	I want you to have an X-ray.
Ume ...	It's ...
-vunjika/-gutuka	broken/sprained
-teguka/-chanika	dislocated/torn
Umeshtua musuli.	You've pulled a muscle.
Nitakupa dawa ya kutoozesha. Sie jambo kubwa.	I'll give you an antiseptic. It's not serious.
Nataka uje tena baada ya siku ...	I want you to come and see me in ... day's time.

DOCTOR

PATIENT

Part 3 — Nervous tension

I'm in a nervous state.	**Nina wasi-wasi.**
I'm feeling depressed.	**Najiona dhaifu.**
I want some sleeping pills.	**Nataka vidonge vya kulala.**
I can't eat/I can't sleep.	**Siwezi kula/Siwezi kulala.**
I'm having nightmares.	**Naona ndoto za kutisha.**
Can you prescribe a ...?	**Unaweza kuniandikia ...?**
tranquilizer	**dawa ya usingizi**
anti-depressant	**dawa ya kutodhoofisha**

DOCTOR

Sehem 3 — Kuwa na wasi-wasi

Unaumia kwa hali ya wasi-wasi.	You're suffering from nervous tension.
Unahitaji kupumzika.	You need a rest.
Vidonge gani vya dawa unatumia?	What pills have you been taking?
Vingapi kila siku?	How many a day?
Muda gani umehisi namna hii?	How long have you been feeling like this?
Nitakuandikia baadhi ya vidonge.	I'll prescribe some pills.
Nitakupa dawa ya kutuliza.	I'll give you a sedative.

PATIENT

Prescriptions and dosage

What kind of medicine is this?	**Dawa ya aina gani hii?**
How many times a day should I take it?	**Niitumie ngapi kila siku?**
Must I swallow them whole?	**Lazima nimeze kidonge kizima?**

Fee

How much do I owe you?	**Gharama yake nini?**
Do I pay you now or will you send me your bill?	**Lazima nilipe sasa au utaniletea hesabu?**
May I have a receipt?	**Unaweza kunipa risiti?**
Thanks for your help, Doctor.	**Asante kwa msaada wako, (Bwana/Bibi)* Daktari.**

DOCTOR

DOCTOR

Utumizi wa dawa

Chukua vijiko ... vya chai vya dawa hii kila saa ...	Take ... teaspoons of this medicine every ... hours.
Chukua vidonge ... pamoja na bilauri ya maji ...	Take ... pills with a glass of water ...
mara ... kila siku	...times a day
kabla ya kula chakula	before each meal
baada ya kula chakula	after each meal
baina ya vyakula	between meals
asubuhi/usiku	in the morning/at night

Malipo

Hiyo shilingi 20, tafadhali.	That's 20 shillings, please.
Tafadhali nilipe sasa.	Please pay me now.
Nitakuletea hesabu.	I'll send you a bill.

*In Swahili, use either "Mr." *(Bwana)* or "Mrs." *(Bibi)* before the title.

FOR NUMBERS, see page 175

Dentist

If you happen to be in the remote parts of East Africa, you can rely on the general practitioner for dental treatment.

Can you recommend a good dentist?	**Unaweza kunisifia daktari mzuri wa meno?**
Can I make an (urgent) appointment to see Doctor ...?	**Naweza kufanya miadi (ya haraka) kumuona Daktari ...?**
Can't you possibly make it earlier than that?	**Huwezi kufanya miadi mapema zaidi?**
I've a toothache.	**Naumwa jino.**
I've an abcess.	**Nina jipu la mdomo.**
This tooth hurts.	**Jino hili linauma.**
at the top at the bottom in the front at the back	**lililo juu lililo chini lililo mbele lililo nyuma**
Can you fix it temporarily?	**Unaweza kutibu kwa muda?**
I don't want it extracted.	**Sitaki ling'olewe.**
I've lost a filling.	**Mjazo wa jino umetoka.**
The gum is very sore	**Ufizi unauma sana**
The gum is bleeding.	**Ufizi unatoka damu.**

Dentures

I've broken this denture.	**Meno yangu ya kubandika yamevunjika.**
Can you repair this denture?	**Unaweza kutengeneza meno haya ya kubandika.**
When will it be ready?	**Lini ya takuwa tayari?**

Optician

In the absence of an optician, the chemist's can take care of your optical requirements.

I've broken my glasses.	**Miwani yangu imevunjika.**
Can you repair them for me?	**Unaweza kunitengenezea?**
When will they be ready?	**Lini itakuwa tayari?**
Can you change the lenses?	**Unaweza kubadilisha vioo?**
I want some contact lenses.	**Nataka miwani ya kubandika machoni.**
I'd like to buy a pair of binoculars.	**Nataka kununua darubini.**
I'd like to buy a pair of sun-glasses.	**Nataka kununua miwani ya jua.**
How much do I owe you?	**Kiasi gani nilipe?**
Do I pay you now or will you send me your bill?	**Nikulipe sasa au utanileta hesabu?**

FOR NUMBERS, see page 175

OPTICIAN

Reference section

Countries

Africa	**Afrika**
Asia	**Asia**
Australia	**Australia**
Burundi	**Burundi**
Canada	**Kanada**
China	**China**
East Africa	**Afrika mashariki**
England	**Uingereza**
Ethiopia	**Ethiopia**
Europe	**Uzunguni [Ulaya]**
France	**Ufaransa**
Germany	**Ujerumani**
Great Britain	**Uingereza**
India	**India**
Ireland	**Ireland**
Italy	**Italia**
Kenya	**Kenya**
Madagascar	**Madagaska**
Malawi	**Malawi**
Mozambique	**Msumbiji**
New Zealand	**New Zealand**
North America	**Amerika kusini**
Rwanda	**Rwanda**
Scandinavia	**Skandinavia**
Scotland	**Skotlandi**
Somalia	**Somalia**
South Africa	**Afrika kusini**
South America	**Amerika kusini**
Spain	**Uspeni**
Sudan	**Sudan**
Switzerland	**Uswisi**
Tanzania	**Tanzania**
Uganda	**Uganda**
USA	**Jumuia ya Amerika**
USSR	**Urusi**
Wales	**Wales**
Zaire	**Zaire**
Zambia	**Zambia**
Zanzibar	**Unguja**

Numbers

0	sifuri	62	sitini na mbili
1	moja	63	sitini na tatu
2	mbili	70	sabini
3	tatu	71	sabini na moja
4	nne	72	sabini na mbili
5	tano	73	sabini na tatu
6	sita	80	themanini
7	saba	81	themanini na moja
8	nane	82	themanini na mbili
9	tisa	83	themanini na tatu
10	kumi	90	tisini
11	kumi na moja	91	tisini na moja
12	kumi na mbili	92	tisini na mbili
13	kumi na tatu	93	tisini na tatu
14	kumi na nne	100	mia
15	kumi na tano	101	mia na moja
16	kumi na sita	102	mia na mbili
17	kumi na saba	110	mia na kumi
18	kumi na nane	120	mia na ishirini
19	kumi na tisa	130	mia na thelathini
20	ishirini	140	mia na arobaini
21	ishirini na moja	150	mia na hamsini
22	ishirini na mbili	160	mia na sitini
23	ishirini na tatu	170	mia na sabini
24	ishirini na nne	180	mia na themanini
25	ishirini na tano	190	mia na tisini
26	ishirini na sita	200	mia mbili
27	ishirini na saba	300	mia tatu
28	ishirini na nane	400	mia nne
29	ishirini na tisa	500	mia tano
30	thelathini	600	mia sita
31	thelathini na moja	700	mia saba
32	thelathini na mbili	800	mia nane
33	thelathini na tatu	900	mia tisa
40	arobaini	1000	elfu moja
41	arobaini na moja	1100	elfu na mia moja
42	arobaini na mbili	1200	elfu na mia mbili
43	arobaini na tatu	2000	elfu mbili
50	hamsini	5000	elfu tano
51	hamsini na moja	10,000	elfu kumi
52	hamsini na mbili	50,000	elfu hamsini
53	hamsini na tatu	100,000	laki moja
60	sitini	1,000,000	milioni moja
61	sitini na moja	1,000,000,000	milioni elfu

first	**kwanza**
second	**pili**
third	**tatu**
fourth	**nne**
fifth	**tano**
sixth	**sita**
seventh	**saba**
eighth	**nane**
ninth	**tisa**
tenth	**kumi**
once	**mara moja**
twice	**mara mbili**
three times	**mara tatu**
half a ...	**nusu**
half of ...	**nusu ya ...**
a quarter	**robo**
one third	**sehemu moja ya tatu [theluthi]**
a pair of ...	**pea moja [jozi]**
a dozen	**dazani**
1985	**mwaka elfu, mia tisa na themanini na tano**
1987	**mwaka elfu, mia tisa na themanini na saba**
1990	**mwaka elfu, mia tisa na tisini**
2000	**mwaka elfu mbili**

Time

When speaking Swahili, time is counted in two 12-hour cycles in East Africa. The daytime cycle begins approximately at sunrise—or 6 a.m., according to our way of expressing time—and ends with sunset—or 6 p.m. Dusk begins a new 12-hour cycle which ends approximately with sunrise, i.e., 6 p.m. to 6 a.m. This means that when we'd say it's 2 p.m., the East African would say it's 8 o'clock in the afternoon, that is, eight hours after the beginning of the daytime cycle commencing with our 6 a.m. On the other hand, if you find yourself invited to dinner at 2 o'clock in the evening, don't be alarmed. That means 8 p.m., according to our way of telling time. Two o'clock simply means two hours after sunset or 6 p.m.

For instance:

6 a.m.	=	12 o'clock	**saa kumi na mbili**
8 a.m.	=	2 o'clock	**saa mbili**
9.30 a.m.	=	3.30	**saa tatu na nusu**
2 p.m.	=	8 o'clock	**saa nane**
noon	=	6 o'clock	**adhuhuri [saa sita]**
midnight	=	6 o'clock	**nusu usiku [saa sita]**

In case the expression isn't clear, add *asubuhi* (daytime cycle) or *jioni* (night-time cycle) at the end of the phrase.

REFERENCE SECTION

REFERENCE SECTION

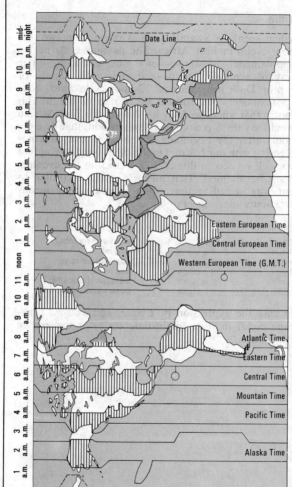

Countries which have adopted a time differing from that in the corresponding time zone. Note that also in the USSR, official time is one hour ahead of the time in each corresponding time zone. In summer, numerous countries advance time one hour ahead of standard time.

Useful expressions

What time is it?	**Saa ngapi sasa?**
Excuse me. Can you tell me the time?	**Samahani. Unaweza kumarifu wakati?**
I'll meet you at ... tomorrow.	**Nitakukuta sar ... kesho.**
I'm sorry I'm late.	**Nisamehe, nimechelewa.**
At what time does ... open?	**... inafungua saa ngapi?**
At what time does ... close?	**... inafunga saa ngapi?**
How long will it last?	**Utaendelea kwa munda gani itakaa?**
What time will it end?	**Itamalizika saa ngapi?**
At what time shall I be there?	**Nitafika kule saa (wakati) gani?**
At what time will you be there?	**Utafika kule saa (wakati) gani?**
Can I come at ... o'clock?	**Unataka niije saa ... ?**
after ... (prep.)	**baadaye**
before ... (prep.)	**kabla**
early	**mapema**
in time	**kwa wakati**
late	**kuchelewa**
hour	**saa**
minute	**ndakika**
second	**nukta**
quarter of an hour	**robo saa**
half an hour	**nusu saa**
afterwards	**badaye**
before	**kabla**

REFERENCE SECTION

FOR NUMBERS see page 175

Days

What day is it today?	**Siku gani leo?**
Sunday	**Jumapili**
Monday	**Jumatatu**
Tuesday	**Jumanne**
Wednesday	**Jumatano**
Thursday	**Alhamisi**
Friday	**Ijumaa**
Saturday	**Jumamosi**
in the morning	**asubuhi**
during the day	**wakati wa mchana**
in the afternoon	**alasiri [adhuhuri]**
in the evening	**jioni [magharibi]**
at night	**usiku**
the day before yesterday	**juzi**
yesterday	**jana**
today	**leo**
tomorrow	**kesho**
the day after tomorrow	**kesho kutwa**
the day before	**juzi**
the next day	**siku nyingine**
two days ago	**siku mbili nyuma**
in three days' time	**baada ya siku tatu**
next week	**wiki ijayo**
for a fortnight (two weeks)	**kwa muda wa wiki mbili**
birthday	**siku ya kuzaliwa**
day	**siku**
day off	**siku ya ruhusa**
holiday	**siku kuu**
holidays	**siku za likizo**
month	**mwezi**
school holidays	**siku za kufungwa skuli**
vacation	**siku za likizo**
week	**wiki**
weekday	**wiki ya kazi**
weekend	**mwisho wa wiki**
working day	**siku ya kazi**

Months

January	**Januari**
February	**Februari**
March	**Machi**
April	**Aprili**
May	**Mei**
June	**Juni**
July	**Julai**
August	**Agosti**
September	**Septemba**
October	**Oktoba**
November	**Novemba**
December	**Desemba**

since June	**tangu Juni**
during the month of August	**katika mwezi wa Agosti**
last month	**mwezi uliopita**
next month	**mwezi ujao**
the month before	**kabla ya mwezi jana**
the next month	**mwezi ujao**

July 1	**tarehe 1 Julai**
March 17	**tarehe 17 Machi**

Due to the vastness of the region and the enormous diversity of climates it encompasses, it's hardly possible to give a single, universally valid breakdown of the seasons. It all depends on where you are!

The local people can identify the season in their own particular area as follows:

msimu wa kaskazi	northern monsoon season
msimu wa kusi	southern monsoon season
miezi ya mvua	rainy season
miezi ya joto	hot season
siku za dharuba	stormy period
siku za baridi	cold period

Public holidays

Here are the official public holidays when schools, offices and shops are closed throughout East Africa.

January 1	**New Year's Day**
May 1	**Labour Day**
December 25	**Christmas Day**
December 26	**St. Stephan's Day**

To the above should be added the movable holidays of Good Friday, and Easter Monday, as well as the Moslem holy days *(Idi)*, the dates of which depend on the lunar calendar. It should also be noted that there may be additional local holidays depending upon the predominant religion of the area.

Below those holidays are given which are peculiar to each East African country.

Uganda

September 1	**Republic Day**
October 9	**Independence Day**

Kenya

June 1	**Constitution Day**
October 20	**Kenyatta Day**
December 12	**Independence Day**

Tanzania

January 12	**Revolution Day**
April 24	**Union Day**
July 7	**Tanganyikan-African National Union (TANU) Day**
December 9	**Independence Day**

National parks and game reserves

Wildlife is one of the major attractions in East Africa. Several reserves are as large as a province. To enter a national park or a game reserve you need a ticket or a permit and you must pay a fee for the car. Picnics and fires are generally prohibited in such areas, with the exception of those parks set aside for campers. Of course, hunting is forbidden, except during certain periods when some parks allow restricted bagging.

Below, you'll find a list of the main reserves and national parks together with the principal animals found in each:

Uganda

Matheniko, Bokora, Pian Upe Game Reserves	antelopes (notably kudu), giraffes, leopards, lions, ostriches, etc.
Kidepo National Park	rhinoceros, buffalo, giraffes, antelopes, elephants, lions, leopards, etc.
Murchison Falls National Park	elephants, antelopes, buffalo, giraffes, lions, leopards, hippopotamuses, crocodiles and many kinds of birds

Kenya

Masai Amboseli Game Reserve	antelopes, zebras, rhinoceros, gnus, cheetahs, leopards, ostriches, some species of birds
Tsavo National Park	the largest park in East Africa; you'll find elephants, antelopes, (notably oryx), buffalo, lions, etc.

Tanzania

Selous Game Reserve	elephants, hippopotamuses, buffalo, gnus, antelopes, (e.g., kudu, elks), lions, leopards
Serengeti National Park	gnus, zebras, antelopes, (impalas, topis and kongonis), Thomson's gazelles, giraffes, lions, cheetahs, leopards

What does that sign mean?

Angalia majibwa	Beware of the dog
Barabara ya mtu pekee	Private road
Baridi	Cold
Dhahabu	Gold
Habari	Information
... hairuhusiwi	... forbidden
Hapana kuingia	No entrance
Hapana kuvuta sigara	No smoking
Hatari	Danger
Hatari ya mauti	Danger of death
Ilani	Notice
Imefungwa	Closed
Imeuzwa	Sold out
Imewekwa	Reserved
Ingia pasipo hodi	Enter without knocking
Kuingia	Entrance
Kuingia bure	Entrance free
Kuna shughuli	Occupied
Kutoka	Exit
Kutoka kwa hatari	Emergency exit
Lifti	Lift (elevator)
Maji gharika	Flood
Maji haya hayafai kwa kunywa	Non-drinkable water
Moto	Hot
Mshika fedha	Cashier's
Njia ya baiskeli	Path for cyclists
Piga hodi (kengele)	Please ring
Sukuma	Push
Taratibu	Caution
Tupu	Vacant
Usiguse	Do not touch
Usivute sigara	No smoking
Uuzaji	Sales
Vuta	Pull
Wanaume	Gentlemen
Wanawake	Ladies
Wapitaji njia wata- hukumiwa	Trespassers will be prosecuted
Ya kukodishwa	To let, for hire
Ya kuuzwa	For sale
Ya mtu pekee	Private

REFERENCE SECTION

Conversion tables

To change centimetres into inches, multiply by .39.

To change inches into centimetres, multiply by 2.54.

Centimetres and inches

	in.	feet	yards
1 mm	0,039	0,003	0,001
1 cm	0,39	0,03	0,01
1 dm	3,94	0,32	0,10
1 m	39,40	3,28	1,09

	mm	cm	m
1 in.	25,4	2,54	0,025
1 ft.	304,8	30,48	0,304
1 yd.	914,4	91,44	0,914

(32 metres = 35 yards)

Temperature

To convert Centigrade into degrees Fahrenheit, multiply Centigrade by 1.8 and add 32.

To convert degrees Fahrenheit into Centigrade, subtract 32 from Fahrenheit and divide by 1.8.

Metres and feet

The figure in the middle stands for both metres and feet, e.g., 1 metre = 3.28 feet and 1 foot = 0.30 m.

Metres		Feet
0.30	1	3.281
0.61	2	6.563
0.91	3	9.843
1.22	4	13.124
1.52	5	16.403
1.83	6	19.686
2.13	7	22.967
2.44	8	26.248
2.74	9	29.529
3.05	10	32.810
3.35	11	36.091
3.66	12	39.372
3.96	13	42.635
4.27	14	45.934
4.57	15	49.215
4.88	16	52.496
5.18	17	55.777
5.49	18	59.058
5.79	19	62.339
6.10	20	65.620
7.62	25	82.023
15.24	50	164.046
22.86	75	246.069
30.48	100	328.092

Other conversion charts

REFERENCE SECTION

Weight conversion

The figure in the middle stands for both kilograms and pounds. e.g., 1 kilogramm = 2.20 pounds and 1 pound = 0.45 kilograms.

Kilograms (kg.)		Avoirdupois pounds
0.45	1	2.205
0.90	2	4.405
1.35	3	6.614
1.80	4	8.818
2.25	5	11.023
2.70	6	13.227
3.15	7	15.432
3.60	8	17.636
4.05	9	19.840
4.50	10	22.045
6.75	15	33.068
9.00	20	44.889
11.25	25	55.113
22.50	50	110.225
33.75	75	165.338
45.00	100	220.450

KASKAZINI
NORTH

MAGHARIBI
WEST

MASHARIKI
EAST

KUSINI
SOUTH

REFERENCE SECTION

Emergency

By the time the emergency is upon you it's too late to turn to this page to find the Swahili for "I'll scream if you…" So have a look at this short list beforehand and, if you want to be on the safe side, learn the phrases shown in capitals.

Be quick	Fanya haraka
Call the police	Ita Polisi
CAREFUL	JIHADHARI!
Come here	Njoo hapa
Come in	Ingia
Danger	Hatari
Fire	Moto
Gas	Gasi
Get a doctor	Ita daktari
Go away	Ondoka
HELP	NISAIDIE(NI)/SAIDIA
Get help quickly	Ita msaada haraka
I'm ill	Ninaumwa [Naumwa]
I'm lost	Nimepotea
I've lost my …	Nimepoteza … yangu
Keep your hands to yourself	Usiniguse!
Leave me alone	Niache
Lie down	Lala chini
Listen	Sikiliza
Look	Angalia
LOOK OUT	JIHADHARI
POLICE	POLISI
Quick	Haraka
STOP	SIMAMA
Stop here	Simama hapa
Stop that man	Msimamishe mtu yule
STOP THIEF	MWIZI
Stop or I'll scream	Niache au nitapiga kelele

FOR CAR ACCIDENTS, see page 150

REFERENCE SECTION

Emergency numbers

Ambulance ....

Fire ....

Police ....

Fill in these as well:

Embassy ....

Consulate ....

Taxi ....

Airport information ....

Travel agent ....

Hotel ....

Restaurant ....

Babysitter ....

....

....

....

....

....

....

Index

Quick reference page

Here are some phrases and expressions which you'll probably need most frequently on your trip:

Please.	**Tafadhali.**
Thank you.	**Asante.**
Yes/No.	**Ndio/Hapana.**
Excuse me.	**Samahani.**
Waiter, please.	**Mtumishi, tafadhali.**
How much is that?	**Hiyo ni kiasi gani?**
Where are the toilets?	**Viko wapi vyoo?**

Choo	Toilets
WANAUME	WANAWAKE

Could you tell me ...?	**Unaweza kuniarifu...?**
where/when/why	**wapi/lini/kwa nini**
Help me, please.	**Tafadhali nisaidie.**
What time is it?	**Saa ngapi sasa?**
one/first two/second three/third	**moja/kwanza mbili/-a pili tatu/-a tatu**
What does this mean? I don't understand.	**Maana ya hii ni nini? Sielewi.**
Do you speak English?	**Unasema Kiingereza?**